CSR AND ITS COMMUNICATION STRATEGIES WITHIN SPAIN'S MARBLE INDUSTRY: AN INTRODUCTION

Mariana Oller Alonso
Martín Oller Alonso

CSR and its Communication Strategies
within Spain's Marble Industry: An Introduction
Mariana Oller Alonso & Martín Oller Alonso

This work has been published by the author through the self-publishing services of EDITORIAL PLANETA, S.A.U. for the distribution and availability to the public under the publishing imprint Universo de Letras; therefore, the author assumes the responsibility for the content therein.

Cover design: Design Team at Universe de Letras

www.universodeletras.com

First edition: 2024

ISBN: 9788410276772
ISBN eBook: 9788410277847

*"It is a reminder
of our shared responsibility
to care for our planet
and a time to reflect
on where we still fall short
of our commitments
to each other."*

António Guterres,
UN Secretary General
(2022)

TABLE OF CONTENTS

INTRODUCTION

Economist Howard R. Bowen first articulated the concept of Corporate Social Responsibility (CSR) in his 1953 book, "Social Responsibilities of the Businessman," where he described it as the duty of business owners to develop corporate policies and make decisions that align with societal goals and values. However, it wasn't until the late 1990s that this idea gained traction in Spain, introduced through the efforts of the Association of Collective Investment Institutions and Pension Funds (INVERCO), which brought the notion of responsible social investment to the Spanish context.

Spain's ongoing challenges with Corporate Social Responsibility (CSR), a concept progressively reshaping our market understanding, highlight he need for this book. It offers an in-depth analysis of CSR within the Spanish marble industry,[1] evaluating companies comprehensive

---

[1] This analysis focuses on environmental considerations and the specific industry in question – in this case, the marble sector. Understanding these facets is vital for grasping the rationale and behavior of managers and executives in these companies, especially concerning communication and Corporate Social Responsibility (CSR) efforts.

communication actions and strategies. This exploration delves into the development and conduct of CSR in the national marble sector, adopting a blended academic and business perspective to bridge the divide between theory and practice.

Is our research proposal relevant? Evidently! Despite hosting some of the most historically significant and globally impactful marble mines, Spain finds itself even further behind in the development of CSR, especially compared to the progress made in other European countries.

For over two thousand years, marble has stood out as a significant natural resource in Spain, utilized by the various cultures and civilizations that have flourished on the Iberian Peninsula. The legacy of their usage is evident in the magnificent architectural, artistic, and craft creations that remain today, evidencing the material's role in propelling indus- trial advancement since antiquity. Marble remains a pivotal force in the mining sector, often called "white gold." The indus- try has transformed from a primarily extractive operation with minimal value addition and a reactive approach to sales to one that fully leverages every production stage. It now captures the "added value" of locally sourced and imported marble, driven by a revolutionary commercial strategy.

Quarry management inherently faces challenges and necessitates a business model that effectively integrates various sector facets, enhancing visibility through improved communication strategies. Despite significant professional practices, technology, and robotics advancements, many operations rely on traditional, outdated production methods. These legacy processes often pigeonhole company identities strictly within extraction, overlooking the potential for developing a more dynamic and recognizable brand image.

As previously discussed, an antiquated communication approach exacerbates the Spanish marble sector's challenges, hindering effective engagement with stakeholders, media, communication platforms, governmental entities, political figures, and customers. This imbalance, further deepened by the economic downturn (2008) and the COVID-19 pandemic (2020), has resulted in annual financial losses for the industry. Therefore, adopting innovative economic and communicative strategies focused on Corporate Social Responsibility (CSR) could present the marble industry with more viable business options. These strategies also have the potential to facilitate a successful generational transition, ensuring the sector's future prosperity.

This book represents a personal dedication, drawing from our extensive experience within the marble sector and international research. It offers a professional and scientific approach, aiming to synergize with the entrepreneurial spirit of marble companies and the support of municipal, provincial, and regional bodies. We strive to provide a catalyst for overcoming the challenges facing Spain's marble industry.

This business remains predominantly driven by personal and family-run companies, now confronting unprecedented challenges pivotal to this work's focus: the imperative to preserve environmental resources, maintain and care for natural stone quarries, and rehabilitate the encompassing ecosystems and communities. Amidst the prevailing health, social, and economic turmoil, the sector struggles to adhere to CSR regulations (e.g., RD 975/2009) within Spain. While technology and digitalization could potentially align the industry with evolving market demands and legal standards, professionals are increasingly burdened by a deficiency in digital expertise and literacy, technological resources (Robotics, Web 3.0, metaverse, and regenerative artificial intelligence stand out as notable examples), and continuous training opportunities.

Through this book, we examine CSR both as an independent domain and a component of the comprehensive communication strategies of Spanish marble enterprises. Despite the growing recognition among extraction firms over the past five years that CSR extends beyond community relations and forms a core aspect of corporate management, there's a noticeable absence of medium—and long-term strategic planning, both internally and externally. Aligning these strategies is essential to ensuring the consistency of all actions undertaken. We believe that once business leaders fully grasp this concept, they will be positioned to enhance their extraction businesses' reputation significantly.

The marble sector is currently facing critical challenges for its survival. Yet, this predicament presents a unique opportunity to demonstrate the societal value of these companies. In the wake of the COVID-19 pandemic, which has triggered widespread health, social, and economic crises, there's a heightened expectation for businesses to engage responsibly and conscientiously. This involves undertaking actions that foster trust and enhance the value of their brands, underpinned by a robust ethical business framework. Now is the moment to embrace learning and turn the tide on this adverse situation, collectively and inclusively.

UNDERSTANDING CORPORATE SOCIAL RESPONSIBILITY (CSR)

The European Union characterizes social responsibility (SR) as an innovative approach to corporate management and stakeholder engagement, integrating a triple bottom line (social, environmental, and financial) into its strategies, policies, and business practices.[2] This concept encompasses various initiatives to influence society and foster companies' sustainable growth. The Global Reporting Initiative (GRI) has just released a detailed implementation guide designed specifically for the mining sector.[3] This guide is intended to assist mining companies in effectively applying GRI standards to ensure that their operations are both sustainable and socially responsible. The newly introduced guidelines offer comprehensive directions on how to report on economic, environmental, and social impacts. This sector-specific

[2] García de Oteyza, M.O. (2012). Fundamentals of socially responsible management. In J.I. Galán Zazo & A. Sáenz de Miera (Eds.), *Reflections on corporate social responsibility in the 21st century* (pp. 89-104). Salamanca, Spain. University of Salamanca.

[3] Global Reporting Initiative. (2024). GRI 14: Mining Sector 2024. Retrieved from https://www.globalreporting.org/media/f4bkhjbh/gri-sector-standard-project-for-mining_faqs-1.pdf

standard represents a significant advancement in enhancing transparency and accountability in the mining industry, aligning with worldwide sustainability objectives.

Following this reasoning, the European Commission's Green Paper describes corporate social responsibility as "the voluntary incorporation of social and environmental considerations into a company's business practices and interactions with stakeholders."[4] This definition aligns with the concept of CSR as a business approach that acknowledges and addresses the effects of a company's operations on stakeholders, local communities, the environment, and society.[5]

Business leaders, including those in the marble mining industry, prioritize CSR with a keen focus on human resources and market conduct,[6] distilled into four critical motives for implementing CSR initiatives: ethical duty, sustainability, adherence to law, and maintaining a solid reputation.[7] We delve deeper, asserting that mere legal compliance does not equate to social responsibility.[8] This is partly because legal

4   European Commission. (2008). *Communication from the Commission: The 2008 Report on Competitiveness in Europe*. Brussels: European Commission. Retrieved from https://eur-lex.europa.eu/LexUriServ/LexUriServ.do?uri=COM:2008:0774:FIN:EN:PDF

5   Jiménez Herrero, L.M., & Leiva, A. (2010). *Green Employment in a Sustainable Economy*. Observatory of Sustainability in Spain. Madrid: Fundación Biodiversidad.

6   Komodromos, M., & Melanthiou, Y. (2014). Corporate reputation through strategic corporate social responsibility: Insights from service industry companies. *Journal of Promotion Management, 20*(4), 470-478.

7   Foote, J., Gaffney, N., & Evans, J.R. (2010). Corporate social responsibility: Implications for performance excellence. *Total Quality Management & Business Excellence, 21*(8), 799-812.

8   Aragón Medina, J., & Rocha Sánchez, F. (2009). The actors of social responsibility: The Spanish case. *Cuadernos de Relaciones Laborales, 27*(1), 147-167.

standards vary across different countries and regions and are subject to change over time.

In the context of how environmentally conscious and responsible consumers perceive companies, initiatives that foster CSR are paramount.[9] These efforts often involve promoting "eco-friendly" or "green" products that support fair trade practices. Furthermore, adopting CSR strategies can shield companies from disputes with the most genuine consumers dedicated to environmental conservation to the extent that some may even boycott products or services failing to meet these criteria.

21st-century corporate social responsibility (CSR) is characterized by its voluntary nature, beyond philanthropy or social marketing, aimed at value creation and integration into stakeholder relationships to impact the community and broader society. It transcends the notion of a mere quality or technique, embodying a holistic management approach grounded in values, ethics, and excellence, all underpinned by a "universal specificity."[10] Thus, the essence of contemporary CSR, and the pivotal challenge for marble industry leaders, lies in discovering strategies that generate value for both the business and society.

---

[9] Lafuente, A., Viñuales, V., Pueyo, R., & Llaría, J. (2003). *Corporate social responsibility and public policies*. Madrid: Ecology and Development Foundation.

[10] Galan, J.I. (2012). Panorama, challenges, and new research trends. In J.I. Galan & A. Sáenz de Miera (Eds.), *Reflections on corporate social responsibility in the 21st century* (pp. 195-213). Salamanca: University of Salamanca Publications.

GENESIS AND DEVELOPMENT
OF CORPORATE SOCIAL RESPONSIBILITY

During the 1910s, the concept of social control in economics began to be systematically explored[11], framing the notion that businesses are responsible for contributing positively to society and that corporate models should directly address community members' needs and aspirations.[12] The 1930s and 1940s saw the initial acknowledgment of corporate leaders' responsibility to support those unable to sustain themselves through conventional employment or commerce,[13] highlighting business leaders' social obligations. David Packard[14] later expanded on this by emphasizing the collective nature of a 'company,' which, by pursuing specific goals beyond individual capabilities, offers a societal contribution.[15]

The foundation of what is now understood as corporate social responsibility originated in the mid-20th century with Howard R. Bowen's 1953 publication, "Social Responsibilities of the

---

[11]   Clark, J.M. (1926). *Social control of business*. Chicago, IL: University of Chicago Press.

[12]   Donham, W.B. (1927). The social significance of business. *Harvard Business Review*, 5(4), 406-419.

[13]   Berle, A.A., Jr. (1932). For whom corporate managers are trustees: A note. Harvard Law Review, 45(8), 1365-1372.

[14]   Packard was an American engineer and entrepreneur. Alongside Bill Hewlett, he co-founded the electronics company *Hewlett-Packard*. Packard proved an expert manager, and Hewlett contributed numerous technical innovations. The company became the world's most extensive electronic testing and measuring device producer. It also emerged as a leading producer of calculators, computers, and laser and inkjet printers.

[15]   Kreps, T. (1940). Measurement of the social performance of business. In K.R. Wright (Ed.), *An investigation of concentration of economic power for the Temporary National Economic Committee, Monograph 7*. Washington, DC: U.S. Government Printing Office.

Businessman." Bowen's work explicitly outlined the duties of business owners to adopt policies, make decisions, and pursue courses of action that align with the goals and values esteemed by society.

During the 1960s, the exploration of the dynamic between the social responsibilities of business leaders, who shape the economic system, and the public's expectations intensified. Social responsibility was seen as a financial entity's public commitment to society and human resources, aiming to ensure their utilization for widespread social objectives rather than just the limited interests of private persons and corporations.[16] This perspective on corporate social responsibility, suggesting that businesses should prioritize broader societal benefits over maximizing shareholder profits, was not without its critics.[17]

Amidst the skepticism, the narrative shifted in the early 1970s with the "Social Responsibility of Business Corporations" report, which marked a departure from the sole focus on economic goals to address social issues that the business sector's initiatives could ameliorate. This report aimed to redefine the corporate entity as a vital component of a diverse society, emphasizing its role as a committed and accountable member within the national framework. This approach was essential for nurturing the fundamental economy and business functions, unleashing the corporation's productive and organizational potential for societal advantage.[18]

---

[16] Frederick, W.C. (1960). The growing concern over business responsibility. *California Management Review, 2*(4), 54-61.

[17] Friedman, M. (1970, September 13). *The social responsibility of business is to increase its profits. The New York Times Magazine.* https://www.nytimes.com/1970/09/13/archives/a-friedman-doc-trine-the-social-responsibility-of-business-is-to.html

[18] Committee for Economic Development

This viewpoint is bolstered by some scholars arguing that commercial enterprises carry responsibilities beyond merely producing and selling goods and services. In line with this, CSR initiatives should envision these entities by their purpose and means of contributing to our social fabric.[19] Some even contend that social responsibility starts where legal obligations end,[20] positing that mere compliance with the law does not equate to social responsibility, as expected of any law-abiding citizen. Similarly, a company that seeks profit maximization within traditional economic frameworks merely fulfills its primary role. True social responsibility, therefore, entails going beyond these foundational expectations.

During these years, views on corporate social responsibility varied widely, from Friedman's perspective, which confined it to generating profits, to the stance of researchers advocating for a proactive and preventative approach to social initiatives undertaken by businesses.[21]

Archie B. Carroll, a prominent figure who continues to influence the field, embraced a holistic view of corporate social responsibility towards the end of the 1970s, defining it as the capacity to fulfill the economic, legal, ethical, and philanthropic expectations society holds for organizations at any given time. He advocated for a corporate social performance model that serves academics and business leaders, aiding the former in navigating the various conceptualizations of CSR in scholarly literature and enlightening the latter on how CSR is

[19] Manne, H., & Wallich, H.C. (1972). The modern corporation and social responsibility. Washington, DC: American Enterprise Institute for Public Policy Research.

[20] Davis, K. (1973). The case for and against business assumption of social responsibilities. *Academy of Management Journal, 16*(2), 312-322.

[21] Sethi, S.P. (1975). Dimensions of corporate social performance: An analytical framework for measurement and analysis. *California Management Review, 17*(3), 58-64.

intrinsically linked to, rather than separate from, a company's economic performance. This approach also enhances the assessment of a company's social responsibilities, facilitating the identification of social issues and selecting response strategies that align with the prevailing context.[22]

Synthesizing the concepts developed up until the 1980s, some scholars define corporate social responsibility as the duty corporations owe to societal stakeholders beyond just shareholders and outside the mandates of law or union agreements, suggesting that their role should extend beyond mere ownership interests.[23] Consequently, the prevailing notion emerged that CSR entails conducting business in a manner that is not only economically viable but also lawful, ethical, and socially beneficial.[24] In the 1980s, the view of CSR through the lens of stakeholder management became prominent, recognizing that a company's stakeholders encompass all individuals and groups who influence "or are influenced by" the company's objectives.[25]

Despite the literature and ideas put forward until the 1990s,[26] it became apparent that discussing a solidified theory of corporate social performance was challenging and potentially risky, as the earlier theoretical and conceptual frameworks had been presented as standalone concepts. During these

---

[22] Carroll, A.B. (1979). A three-dimensional conceptual model of corporate performance. *Academy of Management Review, 4*(4), 497-505.

[23] Jones, T.M. (1980). Corporate social responsibility revisited, redefined. *California Management Review, 22*(2), 59-67.

[24] Carroll, A.B. (1983). Corporate social responsibility: Will industry respond to cutbacks in social program funding? *Vital Speeches of the Day, 49*(19), 604-608.

[25] Freeman, R.E. (1984). *Strategic management: A stakeholder approach.* Boston, MA: Pitman/Ballinger.

[26] Ackerman, R.W., & Bauer, R.A. (1976). *Corporate social responsiveness.* Reston, VA: Reston Publishing.

years, the quest to solidify the understanding and significance of CSR stems from the imperative for businesses to engage with corporate social networks more closely. This need arises from the market's inherent inconsistencies and diversity, coupled with the absence of a unified theory of CSR.[27] Building on the foundational concepts introduced by R. Edward Freeman, various CSR models evolved to encompass a management approach that integrates environmental considerations and stakeholder interests.[28] Consequently, a positive correlation emerges between a company's social and financial outcomes, highlighting that effective corporate performance hinges on strategies that address the needs of all stakeholders.[29]

Approaching the close of the last century, Archie B. Carroll introduced in 1999 a four-tiered pyramid-structured model of corporate social responsibility [economic, legal, ethical, and philanthropic]. This model posits that a company must incorporate all four elements to be deemed socially responsible. Within this framework, what were once termed "discretionary responsibilities" were redefined as "philanthropic responsibilities."

The dawn of the new millennium marked a significant shift in the visibility and recognition of CSR research. The surge in

[27] Ullmann, A.E. (1985). Data in search of a theory: A critical examination of the relationships among social performance, social disclosure, and economic performance of US firms. *Academy of Management Review*, *10*, 540-557.

Belkaoui, A., & Karpik, P.G. (1989). Determinants of the corporate decisions to disclose social information. *Accounting, Auditing & Accountability Journal*, *2*(1), 36-51.

[28] Wood, D.J. (1991). Corporate social performance revisited. *The Academy of Management Review*, *16*(4), 691-718.

[29] Waddock, S., Graves, S.B., & Samuel, B. (1997). The corporate social performance-financial performance link. *Strategic Management Journal*, *18*(4), 303-319.

CSR-related information at that time was part of a strategic effort to influence public opinion and societal perceptions regarding the legitimacy of business organizations. This shift was characterized by social and environmental disclosures driven by public pressure and heightened media scrutiny.[30] During this period, the prevailing view on CSR emphasized that integrating it into corporate processes enhances a company's competitiveness.[31] This involves embedding ethical principles into strategic decision-making, compelling companies to establish comprehensive corporate codes of conduct and adhere to global standards set by independent international bodies.[32]

The issue of CSR becomes particularly intricate when a company faces "negative episodes" stemming from failures in inclusion, ethics, environmental stewardship, and respect for social and human rights.[33] This situation underscores the urgent need to identify effective response strategies that can alleviate the erosion of public trust and safeguard the corporate reputation of many businesses.

The implementation of CSR is influenced by a nation's culture and a company's organizational values.[34] While the

[30] Hooghiemstra, R. (2000). Corporate communication and impression management – New perspectives why companies engage in corporate social reporting. *Journal of Business Ethics, 27*, 55-68.
[31] Porter, M., & Kramer, M. (2002). The competitive advantage of corporate philanthropy. *Harvard Business Review, 80*(12), 56-68.
[32] Carroll, A.B. (2004). Managing ethically with global stakeholders: A present and future challenge. *Academy of Management Executive, 18*(2), 114-120.
[33] Vaaland, T.I., & Heide, M. (2005). Corporate social responsiveness: Exploring the dynamics of 'bad episodes'. *European Management Journal, 23*(5), 495-506.
[34] Maon, F. (2010). Organizational stages and cultural phases: A critical review and a consolidative model of corporate social responsibility development. *Academy of Strategic Management Journal, 12*(1), 39-58.

global application of CSR varies based on interpretation, local factors such as language, culture, politics, economy, and social and institutional structures play a crucial role in shaping its significance across different world regions. The multinational concept of corporate social responsibility goes beyond national boundaries[35] and encompasses two key aspects. The first is the local viewpoint, which integrates CSR principles from national and professional entities. The second aspect considers CSR within the digital realm and e-commerce, viewing national borders as potential obstacles to commercial activities.

While the principles of CSR are relevant to businesses of all sizes, the discourse on its significance often focuses on larger entities due to their heightened visibility and influence.[36] Recent research underscores this trend, revealing that companies with substantial social capital exhibit more pronounced CSR activities.[37] This emphasis on larger organizations impacts the analysis of sectors like marble, predominantly comprising small and medium-sized enterprises (SMEs), thereby excluding a significant portion of the industry from mainstream CSR research.

The outlook for CSR is optimistic, embodying the prevalent version of mindful capitalism. With the global economy on an upward trajectory, the momentum behind CSR is also expected to rise, garnering increasing support worldwide in developed and developing markets. This momentum suggests that CSR

---

[35] Freeman, I., & Hasnaoui, A. (2011). The meaning of corporate social responsibility: The vision of four nations. *Journal of Business Ethics*, *100*(3), 419-443.

[36] Carroll, A.B. (2018). Corporate social responsibility (CSR) and corporate social performance (CSP). In *The SAGE Encyclopedia of Business Ethics and Society* (pp. 1-13).

[37] Jha, A., & Moon, J. (2015). Corporate social responsibility and social capital. *Journal of Banking & Finance*, *60*, 252-270.

will remain an essential business practice, whether in its existing form or with future adaptations.[38] The unforeseen onset of the COVID-19 pandemic post-2020 and its influence on CSR practices globally posed significant challenges, testing the resilience of corporate social responsibility frameworks. Beyond the obligatory or anticipated measures, companies that extended their support to their furloughed workers have been esteemed and rewarded with enhanced loyalty, productivity, and a durable positive reputation in this so-called "new normal" Consequently, businesses' innovative and daring approaches to providing immediate aid will shape their enduring legacy.[39] This pivotal post-pandemic period demands a shift in CSR from mere philanthropy to sustainable practices, focusing on generating economic value through social benefits.[40] In sum, the pandemic presented a unique opportunity for companies to redefine their CSR strategies, potentially making some of the pandemic-induced changes and innovations lasting elements of organizational management and structure[41] [Table 1].

[38] Carroll, A.B. (2015). Corporate social responsibility: The centerpiece of competing and complementary frameworks. *Organizational Dynamics*, 44, 87-96.

[39] Kramer, M.R. (2020). Coronavirus is putting corporate social responsibility to the test. *Harvard Business Review Online*. https://hbr.org/2020/04/coronavirus-is-putting-corporate-social-responsibility-to-the-test

[40] Porter, M.E., & Gehl, K. (2020, September).The political industry [Video].YouTube. https://www.youtube.com/watch?v=-WKyCJdO6kU

[41] Carroll, A.B. (2021). Corporate Social Responsibility: Perspectives on the CSR Construct's Development and Future. *Business & Society*, 60(6), 1258-1278.

Table 1. Origin and evolution of the concept of Corporate Social Responsibility

PERIOD	YEAR	AUTHOR
Before 1950	1926	Clark
	1927	Donham
	1932	Berle
	1939	Packard
	1940	Kreps
From 1950 to 1980	1953	Bowen
	1958	Levitt
	1959	Chalmers
	1960	Frederick
	1970	Friedman
	1971	Committee for Economic Development
	1972	Manne y Wallich
	1973	Davis
	1975	Sethi
	1979	Carroll

Companies are responsible for contributing positively to society.

Businessmen bear responsibility towards their community members.

Corporate executives must ensure the well-being of community members who cannot support themselves.

Businesses contribute to society in ways that extend beyond financial means.

Businessmen bear societal obligations and responsibilities.

Business leaders are responsible for establishing policies, making decisions, and adhering to action plans that align with society's goals and values.

The focus on shareholder value is rooted in the economic framework.

Emerging perspective on social responsibility among businesses and entrepreneurs.

Social responsibility embodies a public commitment to leveraging economic and human resources for widespread societal benefit rather than solely serving the narrow interests of individuals and corporations.

The sole social duty of corporations is to pursue the maximization of shareholder profits.

A social agreement exists between business and society, implying that the purpose of business is to benefit society.

Organizations willingly engage in economic and legal activities that uphold social responsibility.

Social responsibility takes effect beyond legal requirements, focusing on societal benefits that coincide with the company's objectives.

1975 Sethi Corporate actions are adjusted to meet the societal needs of the society in which they are immersed.

A framework encompassing four components — economic, legal, ethical, and philanthropic — is paired with a tripartite perspective that views social responsibility as an amalgamation of social contract and moral stewardship, societal responsiveness, and handling social matters connected to the business.

PERIOD	YEAR	AUTHOR
From 1950 to 1980	1979	Carroll
	1980	Jones
	1984	Drucker
From 1981 to 2000	1984	Freeman
	1985	Wartrick y Cochran
	1991	Wood
	1999	Carroll
	2000	Hooghiemstra
	2003	Schwartz & Carroll
From 2001 to 2023	2005	Vaaland & Heide
	2006	Porter & Kramer
	2008	Dahlsrud
	2010	Maon *et al.*
	2010	Wood
	2011	European Commission

A framework encompassing four components — economic, legal, ethical, and philanthropic — is paired with a tripartite perspective that views social responsibility as an amalgamation of social contract and moral stewardship, societal responsiveness, and handling social matters connected to the business.

The company's voluntary engagement with a broad spectrum of stakeholders.

'Taming the dragon' - Transforming societal issues and demands into business prospects and economic gains, including productive capabilities, job skills, high-quality employment, and overall welfare.

CSR is viewed through the lens of stakeholder management.

A model within an ethical context incorporates principles, procedures, and corporate strategies.

A management approach that incorporates environmental elements and stakeholder involvement.

Social responsibilities are categorized into four types—economic, legal, ethical, and philanthropic—arranged in a pyramid structure with the economic commitment forming the foundation.

CSR is a strategy for managing stakeholder perceptions and views about the company.

CSR encompasses legal, ethical, and economic dimensions.

CSR integrates ethical, environmental, social, and human rights principles.

CSR enhances the competitive edge of businesses.

CSR is a concept shaped by societal norms and lacks a one-size-fits-all definition.

The national culture and corporate ethos significantly influence the evolution and implementation of CSR.

The organization must evaluate its ethical conduct, pinpoint possible improvement opportunities, and relay these findings to its shareholders and stakeholders.

Voluntary incorporation of social and environmental considerations into companies' business practices and stakeholder interactions.

PERIOD	YEAR	AUTHOR
From 2001 to 2023	2012	Becchetti *et al.*
	2013	Lin-Hi & Müller
	2014	Lu y Liu
	2014	Korschun, Bhattacharya & Swain
	2015	Jha & Moon
	2018	Wood, Mitchell, Bradley & Bryan
	2018	Baskentlia, Senb, Duc & Bhattacharya
	2020	Kramer
		Porter
	2021	Carroll
	2023	Changhua Liao

CSR shifts the company's strategic focus from prioritizing shareholder value maximization to emphasizing the fulfillment of stakeholder objectives.

CSR encompasses positive actions and avoiding harmful practices. Avoiding negative actions is essential for reaping the long-term benefits of positive contributions.

A prominent trend of divergence followed by convergence is evident in the evolution of knowledge dissemination in CSR.

CSR focuses on customer needs and their impact on employee job performance.

Companies situated in areas with substantial social capital tend to exhibit higher levels of CSR.

Revisiting Stakeholder Identification and Relevance After 20 Years: Progress, Challenges, and Future Outlook.

How consumers react to and engage with corporate social responsibility initiatives.

The COVID-19 crisis is challenging businesses to demonstrate the significance of their commitment to corporate social responsibility (CSR).

Post-COVID-19, a solid commitment to CSR will be essential for companies aiming to thrive amidst the lasting changes and innovations brought about by the pandemic.

The recognition of corporate social responsibility plays a role in integrating blockchain technology into green supply chains, showcasing enhancements in profitability, corporate earnings, social welfare, and consumer benefits.

FOUNDATIONS OF CORPORATE SOCIAL RESPONSIBILITY

ETHICS

Ethics examines human behavior through a lens that appraises individuals based on their conduct towards themselves and their interactions with others.[42] Consequently, it's pertinent to consider the role of ethics in the marble industry. We firmly believe in its significance, as the moral integrity of the market economy stands as a prime avenue for fostering solidarity among all humans.[43]

A business represents a community where diverse interests converge, all aligned towards shared goals and making decisions under a unified direction that impacts others.[44] In this context, business ethics emphasizes that what matters extends beyond the legal contract to encompass the moral contract and the mutual acknowledgment of valid expectations. These expectations enhance the company's credibility and social legitimacy when appropriately addressed.[45] How a company conducts its operations determines its ability to earn this credibility and legitimacy, creating expectations among stakeholder

---

[42] Fontrodona, J., & Argandoña, A. (2011). An overview of business ethics. *Universia Business Review, 30,* 12-21.

[43] Homann, K. (2016). The moral quality of the market economy. *Documents up for debate.* IDOE, Madrid, Spain. University of Alcalá.

[44] Cortina Orts, A. (2006). CSR and business ethics. In L. Vargas Escudero (Coord.), *Myths and realities of CSR in Spain. A multidisciplinary approach* (pp.109-120). Navarra, Spain: Thomson Civitas.

[45] Cortina Orts, A. (2004). Business ethics: Not just social responsibility. In ÉTNOR Foundation (Ed), *XIV Permanent Seminar on Economic and Business Ethics (2004-2005)* (pp. 7-18). Valencia, Spain: ÉTNOR Foundation.

groups. This process effectively forms a moral contract and acknowledges the various parties involved in the company's operations.[46]

An ethical company generates a public good by creating material wealth, fostering a climate of trust, and contributing to a better society.[47] Ethics should be integral to business operations, underscoring the need for leaders who base their actions on ethical principles. The foundation of all business activities must be ethics rooted in values that advance the common good.[48] A company's ethical nature is contingent on the ethicality of its employees. By cultivating ethical companies and leaders, socially responsible management is achieved.

Companies that operate ethically gain stakeholder support; as they grow, everyone benefits. In contrast, unethical practices can result in a tarnished reputation and resource depletion, leading to shareholders divesting, skilled managers and employees leaving, and customers opting for products from more reputable firms. Managers aiming to foster ethical decision-making and behavior that benefits stakeholders can utilize four ethical principles or guidelines to evaluate the impact of their decisions on stakeholders:[49]

---

[46] García Marzá, D. (2006). Business ethics: A framework for the definition and management of CSR. In L. Vargas Escudero (Coord.), *Myths and realities of CSR in Spain. A multidisciplinary approach*. Navarra, Spain: Aranzadi.

[47] Cortina Orts, A. (2012). Corporate social responsibility and business ethics. In J.I. Galán & A. Sáenz de Miera (Eds.), *Reflections on corporate social responsibility in the 21st century* (pp. 69-88). Salamanca, Spain: University of Salamanca Editions.

[48] Buyolo García, F. (2015). *Humanize the company: Towards a new ethical formation*. Elche, Spain: Bubok Editorial.

[49] Jones, G.R., & George, J.M. (2009). *Contemporary management* (6th ed.). Mexico: McGraw Hill.

A. Utilitarian Principle: An ethical decision is one that maximizes the overall benefit for the most significant number of individuals.
B. Moral Rights Standard: An ethical decision most effectively upholds and protects the essential, inherent rights of the impacted parties.
C. Justice Guideline: An ethical decision is characterized by its fair and equitable distribution of benefits and burdens among individuals and groups.
D. Transparency Test: A decision is considered ethical if the manager can openly discuss it with external parties, allowing society to accept it.

The COVID-19 pandemic has impacted CSR, consumer ethics, and marketing philosophies. These elements should not be viewed merely as challenges, as the pandemic has also presented significant opportunities for companies to engage actively in CSR activities during the crisis, potentially spurring a new phase of long-term CSR evolution. Ultimately, the future of business lies in being ethical, socially responsible, and environmentally conscious – a failure to adapt may mean not surviving at all.[50]

SUSTAINABILITY

In 1987, the Brundtland Report was introduced to the United Nations by the World Commission on Environment and Development. This report was the first to coin the term "sustainable development," defining it as a form of progress that achieves economic expansion and enhances the quality

---

[50] Cortina, A. (2021, March 26). Adela Cortina: The company of the future will be green, socially ethical, or will not be. *Diario Responsable*.https://diarioresponsable.com/noticias/30926-adela-cortina-la-empresa-d el-futuro-sera-verde-social-etica-o-no-sera

of life and social welfare without exhausting the renewable natural resource base or harming the environment. Furthermore, it emphasizes the importance of preserving these resources and the environment for future generations to meet their needs.

Sustainability is defined as a form of development that fulfills current needs without compromising the ability of future generations to meet their own. This presents a significant challenge amidst the pressing existential crises of our era. Therefore, business leaders must break free from prevailing inertia and embrace their role in fostering sustainability.[51]

Sustainability and sustainable development are intertwined with the triple bottom line (TBL) approach. This framework extends a corporation's focus beyond mere economic value, encompassing environmental and social dimensions.[52] It represents a holistic view of a company's impact and responsibility in these three key areas.

These approaches emphasize the necessity of providing a superior quality of life that addresses the needs of today's population without *jeopardizing* the resources available for future generations. Economic leaders must set clear priorities for a sustainable future to achieve this. This involves ensuring that company growth incorporates considerations including water usage, waste production, carbon dioxide emissions, and the working conditions of their workforce.

[51] Bhattacharya, C.B. (2020). Taking ownership of a sustainable future: Three CEOs offer lessons on their pursuit of sustainability. *McKinsey Quarterly*.
[52] Elkington, J. (2004). Enter the triple bottom line. In A. Henriques & J. Richardson (Eds.), *The Triple Bottom Line: Does It All Add Up? Assessing the Sustainability of Business and CSR*. Earthscan: London.

Business owners can now undertake several potential actions to champion sustainability in the post-pandemic world.[53]

Key actions include embracing sustainable business practices, investing in green technologies and renewable energy, enhancing resource efficiency, and fostering a circular economy. Additionally, it's vital to integrate advanced technologies that are revolutionizing the industry. These technologies encompass:

A. Adoption of Renewable Energy Technology: Integrating clean energy sources in marble operations to lower carbon emissions.
B. Advancements in Automation and Robotics: Automated and robotic equipment enhances efficiency and safety in the extraction and processing stages.
C. Utilization of Digital Twins, AI, and Augmented Reality: These technologies can be applied for enhanced management and maintenance, aiding in better decision-making and staff training.
D. Sensor-Driven Management Systems: Implementing sensor technology for more effective monitoring and bolstering operational safety.

Adopting these technological strategies furthers environmental sustainability and is crucial in generating long-term economic value and establishing a robust business reputation. Sustainability has become a fundamental aspect of the technological and *glocal* agenda, prompting a shift towards more responsible and sustainable business practices.

[53] Bhattacharya, C.B. (2020). Taking ownership of a sustainable future: Three CEOs offer lessons on their pursuit of sustainability. *McKinsey Quarterly*.

HUMAN RESOURCES (SOCIETY)

The Global Reporting Initiative (GRI, 2002) defines the social aspect of sustainability as an organization influencing the societal systems where it operates. This social impact can be gauged by examining how the organization affects stakeholders locally, nationally, and globally. Often, these social factors impact the organization's intangible assets, including human capital and reputation. The GRI identifies four categories of indicators to determine an organization's social performance in corporate social responsibility. These indicators focus on adherence to labor practices, human rights, and issues impacting consumers, the community, and various other societal stakeholders:

A. 'Labor Practices and Decent Work' encompasses aspects such as employment and its characteristics, relationships between employees, unions or representative organizations, practices for recording and reporting occupational safety and health, and the amount of training provided to employees across different categories. Regarding these critical points, the increasing prevalence of 'eco-anxiety' or "climate anxiety," as highlighted by Philippe Conus,[54] is significant. Employees anxious about the potential impacts of future climate change may experience feelings of helplessness and guilt, which can affect their view of the organization's commitment to human rights and its responsibility in tackling global challenges.

---

[54] Philippe Conus describes 'eco-anxiety' (climate anxiety) as the feeling of distress over the future consequences of climate change. This anxiety is intensified by a sense of helplessness: those affected feel simultaneously guilty about the situation, victimized by the inaction of political leaders, and powerless to address the problem.

B. 'Human Rights' is determined by the approach and management of policies controlling adherence to international human rights standards, including the freedom of union association, non-discrimination policies, and procedures and programs to address child labor issues. The well-being of everyone in society is essential. In this context, we observe phenomena such as the effects of emerging phenomena like 'eco fatigue,' termed "ecological fatigue" by José Antonio Corraliza,[55] which refers to a form of environmental weariness. This occurs when the public grows disenchanted with environmental dialogue due to the overwhelming burden and exhaustion from ongoing ecological practices. Such fatigue can influence employee motivation and participation in sustainability efforts at work.

C. 'Society' sets forth the management policies for communities that various activities might impact. It includes measures to ensure compliance with the requirements set by the Organization for Economic Cooperation and Development (OECD) for combating bribery and corruption, along with policies on political contributions and initiatives to prevent unfair competition, such as anti-trust measures. Furthermore, the psychological distress known as 'solastalgia,'[56] a term introduced by Glenn Albrecht, is pertinent in this context. Solastalgia describes the emotional pain

---

[55] In an interview with *EFEverde* (https://www.elconfidencial. com/alma-corazon-vida/2011-10-10/ecofatiga-o-el-cansancio-d e-los-ciudadanos-ante-la-responsabilidad-ecologica_321784/) , this professor of Environmental Psychology at the Autonomous University of Madrid asserts that "ecological fatigue" leads the public to disregard persuasive environmental discourse due to an overload of hyper-responsibility.

[56] Australian philosopher Glenn Albrecht defines the psychological disorders that occur in a native population due to destructive changes in their territory, whether because of human activities or climate changes.

experienced due to environmental changes in one's local environment. This can profoundly affect community well-being and the relationship between a company and its local stakeholders. Addressing solastalgia through strong community engagement and environmental restoration initiatives can fortify community bonds and improve the company's social license to operate.

D. 'Product Responsibility' involves safeguarding customer health and safety, ensuring accurate product information and labeling, adhering to voluntary advertising codes, and respecting consumer privacy. Incorporating the management of eco-fatigue and eco-anxiety into product responsibility ensures that marketing and product development strategies do not worsen these issues. Clear communication about the company's environmental impact and its initiatives to combat climate change can help reduce consumer anxiety and foster trust in the brand.

ENVIRONMENTAL RESOURCES

Integrating environmental regulations, a fundamental aspect of corporate social responsibility is considered a bonus for society. The Ibero-American System of Corporate Social Responsibility (SIRSE) highlights standards like ISO 26000,[57] which describe social responsibility as an organization's accountability for the effects of its decisions and activities on society and the environment. This involves ethical and transparent conduct that supports sustainable development, including societal health and well-being. It also considers stakeholder expectations, adherence to relevant laws, alignment with international behavior standards,

---

[57] All the standards mentioned in this section will be elaborated on in greater detail later in the book.

and embedding these principles across all organizational operations and in its external relationships.[58]

Hence, employing tools that incorporate environmental considerations into a company's comprehensive management is crucial. The ISO 14001 standard provides businesses or organizations with a framework for implementing an Environmental Management System. This framework facilitates the creation of a structured approach to environmental protection, adapting to evolving environmental conditions while balancing socioeconomic needs and preventing pollution. Moreover, this standard serves as a foundational step towards embracing additional environmental initiatives (*Ecodesign*, *EMAS*, *Kyoto Protocol*, etc.).

The primary aim of the ISO 14000 series standards is to promote environmental preservation and prevent pollution, all while considering socioeconomic requirements.[59] Educating individuals on environmental matters is crucial because of their potential to alter their value systems, leading to a society characterized by more supportive, cooperative, autonomous, and fair relationships. Environmental education is a central pillar that bridges various fields of knowledge, embodying a continuous learning journey that fosters respect for all life forms. It advocates for the creation of societies that are both socially equitable and ecologically sustainable.[60] This

[58] Eckler, G. (2017, October 26). The importance of the voluntary international standard ISO 26000 for the application of Social Responsibility initiatives. *Ibero-American System of Corporate Social Responsibility (SIRSE)*. http://sirse.info/la-importancia-la-norma-internacional-vo luntaria-iso-26000-la-aplicacion-iniciativas-responsibilidad-social/

[59] Roberts, H., & Robinson, G. (2003). *EMS Environmental Management System Manual, ISO 14001*. Thomson Editores.

[60] Guillén, F.C. (2016). Education, environment, and sustainable development. *Biocenosis, 18*, 72-78.

approach shows that economic criteria can be harmonized with social and ecological standards.[61]

FAIRTRADE, PRODUCT CERTIFICATION, AND RESPONSIBLE CONSUMPTION

Responsible consumption represents an individual's contribution towards sustainability.[62] The essence of Fairtrade lies in the non-profit motive, ensuring that compensation is equitable and supportive. Within this socio-economic framework, producers, intermediaries, and consumers play a pivotal role in upholding corporate social responsibility. This model prioritizes a fair exchange where the pricing reflects the labor and its associated demands and needs rather than merely following market forces. Here, consumers are open to paying slightly more, and intermediaries accept lower profits, ensuring that producers are fairly compensated for their efforts.

Fairtrade aims to foster an alternative trading system that prioritizes the purchase of products adhering to the principles of fair compensation for producers, alongside promoting social values and environmental respect. Through such alternative marketing channels, there's an opportunity to mitigate the full impact of market dynamics on product sales.[63] Certification marks serve as identifiers for fair trade products to consumers and enable producers to access global

---

[61] Cabrera, P. (2002). Questions and answers about fair trade. in P. Cabrera, G. Sichar Moreno, & A. Zamora (Eds.), *Fair Trade: A real alternative?* CIDEAL and SETEM Foundation.

[62] Inglada Galiana, E., & Sastre Centeno, J.M. (2016). Reflections on corporate social responsibility, public responsibility, and environmental sustainability. *Galician Journal of Economics*, 25(3), 5-22.

[63] Krier, J.M. (Ed.). (2001). *The European Free Trade Association Yearbook. The challenge of Fair Trade 2001-2003*. Belgium: EFTA.

markets.[64] Both producers and traders can apply for a "Fair Trade" certification for their products. This mark is issued once it is confirmed that they comply with the standards established by certification authorities organized under the FairTrade Labeling Organizations International (FLO) and the requisite licensing fees are paid.[65]

In adopting this approach, consumers engage in conscious and responsible consumption, selecting products based on quality and price and considering the products' origins and the companies' practices. The core idea behind accountable and conscious consumption is the recognition that every individual shares responsibility for the social and ecological impacts of production.[66]

While CSR is often viewed as static, the current heightened crisis highlights its dynamic nature. This evolving aspect challenges not only marble companies but all types of businesses to understand consumer ethical choices shaped by the COVID-19 crisis. However, there's room for cautious optimism as the ethical aspect of consumer decision-making has gained prominence during the pandemic, likely shifting towards more responsible and prosocial consumption patterns. These anticipated shifts are expected to influence the operations of companies and organizations significantly.[67]

---

[64] Cabrera, P. (2002). Questions and answers about fair trade. in P. Cabrera, G. Sichar Moreno, & A. Zamora (Eds.), *Fair Trade: A real alternative?* CIDEAL and SETEM Foundation.
[65] Buendía Martínez, I., Coque Martínez, J., & García Alonso, J.V. (2007). Fair Trade: Ethics in business relationships within a globalized environment. *Idelcoop Magazine, 34*(179), 306-323.
[66] Orozco Martínez, S. (2000). *Fair Trade, responsible consumption.* Intermón.
[67] He, & Harris. (2020). The impact of Covid-19 pandemic on corporate social responsibility and marketing philosophy. *Journal of Business Research, 116*, 176-182. https://doi.org/10.1016/j.jbusres.2020.05.030

REGULATION, STANDARDIZATION, AND LEGISLATION OF CSR IN SPAIN

In Spain, the regulatory body for Corporate Social Responsibility (CSR) is the *State Council for Corporate Social Responsibility* (CERSE). Established on January 20, 2009, this advisory and consultative organization is affiliated with the Ministry that oversees public policies to encourage and advance companies' CSR initiatives within the Spanish Government.

The establishment of the CERSE is designed to consolidate representatives from various stakeholder groups involved in corporate social responsibility within a single entity. CERSE leadership and administrative functions include its organization, technical support, and management activities, which fall under the Ministry of Labor, Migration, and Social Security jurisdiction, as well as the *General Directorate of the Autonomous Work*, Social Economy, and Corporate Social Responsibility, respectively.

The latter oversees corporate social responsibility as per Royal Decree 343/2012 of February 10, which outlines the basic organizational structure of the *Ministry of Employment and Social Security*. This includes primarily promoting CSR among small and medium-sized enterprises (SMEs) and designing, processing, and overseeing programs to disseminate and enhance CSR in businesses—a crucial aspect for sectors like marble. Moreover, the *State CSR Council* serves an informative role regarding public initiatives and regulations that influence the practices of companies, organizations, and public and private institutions, fostering legal compliance and contributing to social and economic development.

Recent modifications in the framework and functioning of CERSE have enhanced its capacity to tackle contemporary social responsibility and sustainability challenges effectively.[68] The *Spanish Corporate Social Responsibility Strategy*, established in 2014, continues to serve as a pivotal national guideline, incorporating 60 actions to foster responsible conduct within public and private entities.[69] CERSE has also updated its practices to align with the *United Nations Sustainable Development Goals* (SDGs), explicitly promoting equality and socio-environmental sustainability.[70] This adaptation includes a new set of rules that modernize its governance and operations, now integrating a gender perspective.[71] CERSE has developed

[68] The Law. (2021). The government promotes the State Council for Corporate Social Responsibility. https://www.elderecho.com

[69] Ministry of Inclusion, Social Security and Migration. (n.d.). The Plenary Session of the CERSE approves the Spanish Strategy for Corporate Social Responsibility. Retrieved from https://www.inclusion.gob.es

[70] Ibercampus. (2021). Renewed the State Council for Corporate Social Responsibility (CERSE) to meet the SDGs. Retrieved from https://www.ibercampus.es

[71] Ministry of Labor and Social Economy. (n.d.). State Council for Corporate Social Responsibility (CERSE). Retrieved from https://www.mites.gob.es

multiple documents and formed working groups to address various CSR issues more comprehensively, showcasing its proactive and thorough approach to examining and analyzing social responsibility matters.

In Spain, following the guidance of the European "Green Book," the *Parliamentary Subcommittee on Social Responsibility* of the *Congress of Deputies* released the "White Paper" on Corporate Social Responsibility in 2006. This document aimed to foster, encourage, and manage CSR within the country, targeting businesses, public organizations, and other interest groups.

Likewise, in line with directives from the *European Commission*, the Spanish government ratified the *Spanish Strategy for Corporate Social Responsibility* (Strategy 2014-2020) on July 16, 2014, through the plenary session of CERSE and subsequently on October 24 by the *Council of Ministers*. Serving as a benchmark for social responsibility, this strategy encompasses 60 measures designed to encourage the adoption of responsible practices in both public and private organizations. The primary goal is to create a significant impetus for the nation's competitiveness and steer it towards a more productive, sustainable, and inclusive society and economy.

This document outlines the Spanish CSR strategy based on six core principles: competitiveness, social cohesion, shared value creation, sustainability, transparency, and voluntariness. It is guided by four strategic objectives: A) To encourage and advance CSR in Spain. B) To recognize and advocate for CSR as a critical factor in competitiveness, sustainability, and social cohesion. C) To disseminate CSR values across society. D) To establish a unified reference framework for business practices nationwide through various action plans. The strategy encompasses ten action lines, each with specific measures to boost Spanish competitiveness.

Following this action, the National Action Plan for Business and Human Rights was adopted on July 28, 2017. This plan mirrors the implementation of the United Nations Guiding Principles on Business and Human Rights in Spain. It embodies a commitment to safeguarding these rights against any adverse effects arising from business activities and to offer effective remedies for those affected.

The government's goals include identifying and mitigating risks to enhance sustainability and boost the confidence of investors, consumers, and society at large. Secondly, there is an emphasis on increasing the disclosure of non-financial information, particularly in social and environmental domains.

The recently enacted *Non-Financial Information Law*[72] in Spain passed towards the end of 2018, mandates that companies employing over five hundred workers and classified as being of public interest or those having an annual turnover exceeding forty million euros or assets above twenty million euros are required to submit a comprehensive report on their CSR policies. This report and their Annual Accounts must be filed in the Commercial Registry. In this report, organizations/companies are required to compile and disclose their information in two main sections: The first section encompasses details about the company's management practices, while the second section is dedicated to outlining the impact (containing environmental, social, human rights, anti-corruption measures, and societal effects) that the company has on its surroundings. On July 5, 2024, the

---

[72] Official State Gazette. (2018, December 28). https://www.boe.es/eli/es/l/2018/12/28/11/dof/spa/pdf

definitive version of Directive (EU) 2024/1760 on corporate sustainability due diligence was released. This directive imposes requirements on large enterprises concerning human rights and environmental protection, applying to their subsidiaries and business partners. (Publications Office of the European Union, 2024)[73]

Like the previous example, significant updates have been made to Spain's laws and regulations governing non-financial reporting up to 2024. These updates particularly pertain to Directive 2014/95/EU, the *Non-Financial Reporting Directive* (NFRD),[74] and the newly implemented *Corporate Sustainability Reporting Directive* (CSRD).[75]

The Non-Financial Information Law, enacted in Spain at the end of 2018, and its subsequent updates changed the country's CSR landscape. However, this was just the initial step. The introduction of the CSRD Directive 2022/2464/EU, which will be applicable for reporting from 2024, establishes a unified digital format and disclosure standards known as the *EU Sustainability Reporting Standards* (ESRS). Additionally, this Directive shifts the terminology from "non-financial information" to "sustainability information," indicating a move towards enhanced sustainability and transparency in corporate reporting. This regulatory evolution closely aligns with the objectives of the CSDDD (Corporate Sustainability Due Diligence Directive) or CS_3D (Corporate Sustainability

[73] Publications Office of the European Union. (2024, July 5). Official Journal L series daily view. EUR-Lex. https://eur-lex.europa.eu/oj/daily-view/L-series/default.html?&ojDate=05072024

[74] Official Journal of the European Union. (2014). Directive 2014/95/eu of the European parliament and of the council. https://eur-lex.europa.eu/eli/dir/2014/95/oj

[75] Official Journal of the European Union. (2022). Directive (eu) 2022/2464 of the european parliament and of the council. https://eur-lex.europa.eu/legal-content/ES/TXT/HTML/?uri=CELEX:32022L2464

Directive), which promotes the integration of environmental, social, and governance (ESG) criteria into business practices. The CSDDD/CS3D aims to ensure that European companies take responsibility for their impacts in these areas and foster sustainability throughout their value chains. Therefore, introducing common disclosure standards as part of the CSRD aligns with the broader goals of the EU regarding corporate sustainability and transparency.[76]

Comparative analyses on an international scale show distinct differences in CSR disclosure practices across various sectors. A study on the UK's 2017 KPMG survey found that CSR reporting levels in the extractive industry are notably higher than in the retail sector. Additionally, this research underscores the effect of board composition on CSR disclosure, establishing a positive relationship between disclosure levels and aspects like board gender diversity, independence, and size. These results underscore how corporate attributes can influence CSR activities and provide critical perspectives for understanding the disparities in CSR dissemination across different economic environments and sectors (Wang et al., 2022).[77]

To summarize, companies can embed sustainability into their core operations through the framework of the Non-Financial Reporting Law in Spain and its updates. As emphasized by Luz Castillas, the general secretary of the Spanish green growth

---

[76] Chao Janeiro, M. (2024, February 9). Up to Date on Sustainability [Sustainability Update]. LinkedIn. Retrieved March 28, 2024, https://www.linkedin.com/pulse/al-d%2525C3%2525ADa-en-sostenibilidad-monica-chao-janeiro-hylnf/?trackingId=yrBkAEna To2L1V8JIV1uFA%3D%3D

[77] Wang, Y., Yekini, K., Babajide, B., & Kessy, M. (2022). Antecedents of corporate social responsibility disclosure: Evidence from the UK extractive and retail sector. *International Journal of Accounting & Information Management*. https://www.emerald.com/insight/1834-7649.htm

group,[78] green growth presents a significant opportunity for Spanish companies, thus highlighting the importance of these matters reaching the *Board of Directors*. Boards must develop adequate sustainability competencies to mitigate risks and capitalize on opportunities.

In the Andalusian region, responsibility for promoting CSR does not fall under a single department or entity within the *Junta de Andalucía*. Instead, tasks related to CSR are spread across multiple departments and agencies. Notably, the *General Directorate of Labor Relations and Occupational Health and Safety* is responsible for coordinating the following aspects:

- The *Ministry of Finance and Public Administration* oversees integrating social clauses into public contracts within the Andalusian region. These clauses, encompassing social and environmental considerations, are incorporated into procurement procedures to enhance labor conditions, safeguard the environment, improve resource efficiency, combat inequality, and foster innovation.
- The *Ministry of Employment, Business, and Commerce* plays a crucial role in facilitating the employment of individuals facing social disadvantages or those at risk of exclusion, utilizing the Andalusian Employment Service for this purpose. Entry into the workforce is seen as a critical method for achieving true social inclusion and preventing the marginalization of these groups. In this scenario, businesses emerge as crucial entities for promoting employment integration. The Junta de

---

[78] Vigario, A. (2019, April 23). Non-financial information law: The company integrates sustainability. *El Economista.* https://www.eleconomista.es/energia/noticias/9837792/04/19/Ley-de-inf ormacion-no-financiera-la-empresa-integra-la-sostenibilidad.html

Andalucía and Obra Social "la Caixa" are advancing the *Incorpora Program* to ease the job entry process for people with significant challenges.

- The *Ministry of Economy and Knowledge* is tasked with advancing CSR among the self-employed and the social economy sector, facilitated by the *Directorate-General of Social Economy and Self-Employed*. Additionally, it supports entrepreneurs through the *Andalucía Emprende Public Foundation*.
- The *Ministry of Equality and Social Policies* oversees initiatives to encourage the development of equality plans and the balance between professional and family life, with a specific focus on the efforts of the *Andalusian Women's Institute*.
- The *Ministry of Environment and Territorial Planning* is tasked with fostering exemplary business conduct through its portal dedicated to climate change and environmental volunteering.

The *Ministry of Labor, Migration, and Social Security* of Spain (2020) highlights corporations' and various organizations' societal and environmental responsibilities. It details a collection of guides, standards, and global regulatory tools designed to assess social responsibility and sustainability performance across various institutions, which are introduced in the subsequent text:

- *United Nations Global Compact*

    This initiative encompasses four critical domains: human rights, labor standards, environmental protection, and anti-corruption. It catalyzes companies and organizations to contribute towards the *United Nations' Sustainable Development Goals* (SDGs), a strategic framework aimed at benefiting people, the planet, and prosperity through to 2030. This approach marks a renewed pursuit of corporate social responsibility, urging businesses and communities at both local and international levels to embrace change. In Spain, entities possessing a *Spanish CIF* and employing more than nine individuals are encouraged to align their goals by becoming signatory partners or engaging even further as participating partners.

- *OECD Guidelines for Multinational Enterprises*

These guidelines ensure alignment between corporate operations and governmental policies, with the following objectives: A) Ensure that corporate actions align with public strategies. B) Enhance the bond between businesses and the communities where they operate. C) Foster an appealing environment for international investment. D) Boost the role of businesses in global sustainable development efforts. The principles outlined offer voluntary guidelines and standards for ethical business practices that align with internationally accepted laws and norms.

- *Tripartite Declaration of the International Labor Organization (ILO)*

This provides companies with advice on adopting social policies and practices that are inclusive, responsible, and sustainable in the workplace. Originating from the *Treaty of Versailles*, which concluded the First World War in 1919, the *International Labour Organization* (ILO) became the first specialized agency of the *United Nations* dedicated to labor issues in 1946. A century later, with 187 member countries, the ILO boasts a distinctive structure that unites government, employer, and worker representatives. It sets global labor standards, advocates for workplace rights, supports the development of decent work opportunities, enhances social protection, and fosters dialogue on work-related matters relevant to the 21st century.

- *United Nations Guiding Principles on Business and Human Rights*

  Adopted by the *United Nations* in 2011, these guidelines are organized around three core pillars: A) The State's duty to respect, protect, and fulfill human rights and fundamental freedoms, encompassing political, judicial, and regulatory spheres. B) Businesses must adhere to established norms and laws, with repercussions for non-compliance. C) The State and businesses' commitment to provide appropriate and effective redress in instances of violations.

- *Global Reporting Initiative* (GRI)

  This entity is a self-governing international body dedicated to formulating standards in environmental protection, anti-corruption, human rights, and labor practices. It assists companies, governments, and various organizations generate sustainability reports, enabling them to understand and disclose their impacts on critical sustainability topics, such as climate change, human rights, governance, and social welfare.

  The Global Reporting Initiative (GRI) employs four strategic methods to achieve its goals: A) Developing standards and guidelines to foster sustainable development. B) Streamlining the sustainability reporting landscape. C) Leading in the creation of efficient and effective sustainability reports. D) Encouraging sustainability data to enhance organizational performance, genuinely contributing to a broad range of stakeholders, all serving the public good.

- *Integrated Reporting* (IR)

  This process elucidates the connections between an organization's strategy, governance, and financial outcomes and its social, economic, and environmental context. Annually, at the *World Economic Forum* in Davos, Switzerland, leading companies, institutions, and global figures convene to advocate for a cohesive and sustainable future. On January 21, 2020, the *International Integrated Reporting Council* (IIRC) unveiled a novel framework for integrated thinking to foster long-term, sustainable decision-making. This approach empowers businesses to fulfill their roles as stakeholders committed to a sustainable future. The model was collaboratively crafted by over fifty entities globally, including notable organizations such as *BASF, HSBC, Solvay, Standard Bank*, and *ING*.

- *European Sustainability Reporting Standards (ESRS)*

The *European Union Sustainability Reporting Standards* (ESRS) introduce a framework of disclosure and compliance obligations for EU businesses exceeding certain size thresholds: more than 250 employees, annual revenues over €40 million, or total assets above €20 million. Additionally, it encompasses international corporations generating more than €150 million annually within the EU, provided they operate at least one subsidiary or branch in the EU meeting specific criteria. The ESRS aims to enhance the precision, uniformity, consistency, comparability, and standardization of corporate sustainability and environmental social governance reporting. As a modification of the existing *EU Non-Financial Reporting Directive*, this framework has been enforced throughout the EU since 2023, with a phased approach to adopting these sustainability reporting standards.

The primary objective of the ESRS is to mitigate corporate *greenwashing* by standardizing and formalizing sustainability reporting practices for companies.

Comprising twelve sections, the ESRS covers a range of areas, including overarching principles, strategy, governance, materiality assessment, and detailed guidelines for reporting on environmental, social, and governance issues. It mandates that companies align the reporting period of their sustainability reports with the timeframe used for their financial statements.

- *AA1000 AccountAbility*

This approach serves as a mechanism for ensuring the integrity of evaluations and the dissemination of information on corporate management's social and ethical dimensions. *Accountability* is an international organization specializing in sustainability standards and consultancy, collaborating with corporations, governmental bodies, and multilateral institutions to foster ethical business conduct. The AA1000 standards are founded on fundamental principles: A) Inclusiveness, ensuring individuals have a say in decisions impacting them. B) Materiality, requiring entities to identify and communicate clearly on critical sustainability concerns. C) Responsiveness obligates organizations to address sustainability issues and their effects transparently. D) Impact, demanding that organizations take responsibility for and measure the effects of their actions on their wider surroundings.

- *ISO 26000:2010* (Social Responsibility)

This represents a globally recognized voluntary guide for best practices in social responsibility, structured around seven key areas: corporate governance, human rights, labor practices, environmental stewardship, ethical business practices, consumer rights, and community involvement. It underpins the endeavors of businesses and organizations striving to act in the most socially responsible manner for the benefit of society.

Unlike certifiable standards such as ISO 9001:2015 and ISO 14001:2015, ISO 26000 is a non-certifiable, voluntary guideline.

- *ISO 9001:2015* (Quality Management)

This standard equips small and medium-sized enterprises (SMEs) with the tools to compete equally with more giant corporations. ISO 9001, crafted by the *International Organization for Standardization* (ISO), outlines a methodology designed to enhance the quality of products and services. It applies to the *Quality Management Systems* of public and private organizations, irrespective of their size or the nature of their business. The latest version, ISO 9001:2015, was released on September 23, 2015, superseding ISO 9001:2008.

- *ISO 14001:2015* (Environmental Management)

This guide provides a framework for systematically addressing the environmental impacts of all activities within an organization or company. It is a foundational tool for demonstrating leadership in aligning an organization's Environmental Management System with prevailing regulations. The critical advancements introduced by this standard can be distilled into five main points: A) Enhanced engagement and involvement from top management. B) Increased integration into business strategies. C) Enhanced focus on environmental conservation. D) Adoption of a life cycle perspective. E) Improved communication effectiveness.

- *Community Environmental Management and Audit System* (EMAS)

This voluntary instrument, devised by the *European Commission*, facilitates the registration and public acknowledgment of enterprises and institutions that have adopted an environmental management system, enabling them to assess, manage, and enhance their environmental impact. Participants in EMAS, varying in administrative, commercial, and ownership characteristics, adopt unified policies as outlined in a verified environmental statement, which sets forth several stipulations: A) A pledge to enhance their environmental practices. B) The establishment of transparent communication. C) Employee engagement. D) The issuance of an EMAS environmental statement. E) The execution of an environmental review. F) Registration with an authoritative entity following successful verification.

- *SA 8000:2014 (Social Accountability)*

The SA8000 certification, developed by Social Accountability International (SAI), is a voluntary accreditation to enhance working conditions, including social justice and workers' rights. It is recognized by leading corporate and industry representatives for its strict standards that ensure top quality in the social compliance of supply chains while also accommodating commercial interests. Organizations holding the SA8000:2014 certification must establish a Health and Safety Committee that includes representatives from management and the workforce.

- *SGE 21 Foretica*

This refers to the *Ethical and Socially Responsible Management System*, marking the first European standard that defines the criteria organizations and companies must adhere to for incorporating social responsibility into their strategic and managerial frameworks. It is crucial for embedding environmental, social, and governance principles, mandating organizations' adoption, and assessing the Ethical and Socially Responsible Management system.

- *IQNet SR10 or "Social Responsibility Management Systems"*

This specification outlines the criteria for a social responsibility management system tailored to organizations that adhere to sustainable development principles and social responsibility recommendations. Crafted by the international IQNet certificate network, it compiles best practices and advice concerning social responsibility. Its advantages stem from enhancing the sustainability of economic, environmental, social, and governance factors in connection with various stakeholders. Consequently, it elevates companies' trust, credibility, and societal reputation.

Acknowledging the impracticality of cataloging every global organization or initiative that focuses on the social responsibility of companies and organizations, we offer a selection of illustrative examples:

- Founded in 1995 and headquartered in Geneva, Switzerland, the *World Business Council for Sustainable Development* (WBCSD)[79] is an organization dedicated to corporate social responsibility focusing on sustainable development. It employs a science-based strategy to drive sustainable growth by identifying business solutions that enhance commercial success. To achieve its Sustainable Development Goals, WBCSD mandates the adoption of six key program areas: A) Circular economy, B) Cities and mobility, C) Climate and energy, D) Food and nature, E) Redefining value to measure and manage risk, and F) People.
- Launched in the United Kingdom in 1998 by a coalition of businesses and organizations, primarily from the food, beverage, and textile industries, the *Ethical Trading Initiative* (ETI)[80] was established as a code of conduct to oversee and ensure good social practices.

---

[79] World Business Council for Sustainable Development (WBCSD). (n.d.). Retrieved from https://www.wbcsd.org/
[80] Ethical Trading Initiative. (n.d.). Retrieved from https://www.ethical-trade.org/

Its membership encompasses global corporations with extensive supplier networks, international trade unions, specialized labor rights groups, and development NGOs. As of 2020, ETI's strategic vision aims to position itself and its members as leaders in ethical trading, emphasizing the importance of transparency in operations and accountability for their commitments.

- Since its inception in 1989, the Clean Clothes Campaign (CCC)[81] has been at the forefront of a worldwide effort to enhance labor conditions and empower workers within the global garment and sportswear sectors. CCC is committed to upholding fundamental labor rights, educating and engaging consumers, applying pressure on corporations and governmental bodies, and providing direct support to workers advocating for their rights and improved working environments. As a coalition, CCC unites various unions and non-governmental organizations focused on multiple issues, including women's rights, consumer protection, and alleviating poverty. Operating as a vast network of numerous organizations and unions across both the manufacturing and consumer ends of the garment industry, CCC identifies local challenges and goals, translating them into worldwide initiatives and crafting campaign strategies to assist workers in meeting their objectives.

- The Initiative for the *Assurance of Responsible Mining* (IRMA)[82] provides a comprehensive framework to promote ethical and sustainable mining activities worldwide. This initiative emphasizes several vital principles, including operational transparency, human rights adherence, environmental stewardship, community engagement,

---

[81] Clean Clothes Campaign. (n.d.). Retrieved from https://clean-clothes.org/

[82] Initiative for Responsible Mining Assurance. (n.d.).https://responsi-blemining.net/

fair and safe labor practices, and the establishment of responsible and ethical supply chains. These supply chains prevent conflict financing and ensure legality and transparency in mineral extraction and trading. IRMA has emerged as a leading standard for mining entities committed to showcasing their commitment to ethical and sustainable mining operations. By adhering to IRMA's guidelines, mining companies safeguard the environment, enhance the quality of life for communities affected by mining activities, and align their operations with globally recognized ethical standards. This initiative provides a structured approach for mining companies to conduct their business responsibly and transparently.

- The International *Council on Mining and Metals* (ICMM)[83] is a pivotal organization that unites leading mining and metals sector entities to enhance the industry's sustainability performance. Created to address significant sustainability issues within mining, ICMM is dedicated to advancing practices that lessen adverse effects while amplifying social and economic advantages. Its primary focus areas are: (1) Workplace Safety: Advocating for stringent safety protocols and exchanging best practices to diminish risks in the workplace. (2) Environmental Stewardship: Encouraging environmental and biodiversity preservation alongside the prudent management of natural resources. (3) Community Rights: ICMM emphasizes the importance of honoring the rights of indigenous and local communities, ensuring practices such as free, prior, and informed consent are upheld.

ICMM is committed to fostering transparency and accountability, collaborating with governments, NGOs,

---

[83] The International Council on Mining and Metals. (n.d.). Retrieved from https://www.icmm.com/

and local communities to promote these principles within the mining and metals industry.

- The *Extractive Industries Transparency Initiative* (EITI)[84] represents a worldwide benchmark for the sound governance of oil, gas, and mineral resources, with a core emphasis on fostering transparency and accountability within the extractive industry. EITI's key characteristics include (1) Financial Transparency: Mandates that both public and private sector entities reveal details regarding their payments while requiring governments to disclose their revenues. (2) Multi-Stakeholder Involvement: EITI stands as a collaborative effort among governments, corporations, and civil society organizations, all aimed at enhancing governance practices. (3) Efficient Revenue Utilization: Aims to guarantee that income from natural resources is allocated effectively towards promoting sustainable development.

  EITI supports open dialogue and cooperation among all parties involved, contributing to improved governance standards in countries abundant in natural resources.

CORPORATE SOCIAL RESPONSIBILITY ACTIVITIES IN SPAIN

Various initiatives involving agreements, partnerships, and conventions have been implemented to create a more competitive, productive, sustainable, and inclusive Spanish society and economy. A prime illustration of this movement is the partnership agreement aimed at fostering *Socially Responsible Investment* (SRI), which was inked in April 2016 between the Spanish *Ministry of Employment and Social*

---

[84] The Extractive Industries Transparency Initiative. (n.d.). Retrieved from https://eiti.org/

Security (MEYSS)[85] and the *Spanish Socially Responsible Investment Forum* (SPAINSIF).

As per the Spanish MEYSS, this agreement and other initiatives aim to equip businesses and administrative bodies with various tools to incorporate, share, and oversee ethical, environmental, social, human rights, and governance standards within their investment strategies for financial and savings products. The goal is to encourage socially responsible investment practices among investors of all sizes. This approach supports social entrepreneurship by advocating for sustainable economic, social, and environmental initiatives that embody the core principles of good governance in investment decisions.

In Spain, CSR is shifting towards a business model prioritizing social impact, marked by increased investments directed towards sustainability, inclusivity, and retaining talent.[86] In the face of the health crisis, businesses have adopted a more human-centric approach to management, focusing more on their workforce's physical and mental well-being. The shift towards remote work has led to adopting more flexible working arrangements, enhancing work-life balance. Moreover, there's been a notable increase in community solidarity and support for small enterprises, showcasing a solid commitment to local development and community welfare. Efforts to facilitate the employment of individuals with disabilities have also intensified, aiming for greater workplace diversity and inclusion.

---

[85] Spanish Ministry of Employment and Social Security. (n.d.). Retrieved from http://www.mitramiss.gob.es/

[86] SAP Spain. (2021, September). *Upcoming trends in corporate social responsibility in Spain.* https://news.sap.com/spain/2021/09/proxima s-tendencias-en-responsibilidad-social-corporativa-en-espana/

During the COVID-19 pandemic, the significance of social impact and volunteering surged, particularly in aiding the healthcare, social services, and education fields. Corporate volunteering expanded, with more employees participating in social initiatives. Furthermore, CSR efforts created sustainable job opportunities within sectors like renewable energy and the circular economy, establishing Spain as a leading market for Socially Responsible Investment (SRI) in Europe. On both European and international stages, Spain has emerged as a frontrunner in the field of CSR, engaging in global initiatives and enacting robust CSR laws. The country has earned international acclaim for its emphasis on innovation and sustainable growth, earning it a place on global sustainability indices.

In this field, which the Spanish government initiated, additional initiatives like *Enterprise 2020*[87] have emerged. This corporate collaboration project is the sole initiative endorsed by the *European Commission's European Social Responsibility Strategy*, spearheaded by Forética in Spain since 2011. This initiative seeks to foster the promotion and spreading of exemplary CSR practices through a joint effort led by businesses. Despite the launch of numerous campaigns and cooperative ventures from its start, it wasn't until November 2015 at the *Enterprise 2020* Summit that the *European Youth Pact* was unveiled. This pact is dedicated to enhancing collaborations between businesses and educational institutions to improve employability, skill development, and the integration of young individuals.[88]

---

[87] Seres Foundation. (n.d.). *The evolution of CSR in Spain through the social impact of our companies.* https://www.fundacionseres.org/BlogSeres/index.php/la-evolucion-la-rsc-espana-traves-del-impacto-social-nuestras-empresas/

[88] Forética. (n.d.). *Enterprise 2020.* https://www.foretica.org/presentacion_enterprise_2020.pdf

In the closing years of the first decade of the 21st century, specifically on April 15, 2008, the *Retos*[89] national network was launched. Its core mission is centered on the formulation, integration, and execution of strategies aimed at fostering socially responsible regions, thereby enhancing the living standards of their populations. Over the past five years, a notable initiative has been the "Agenda 2030 for Sustainable Development," endorsed by the *UN General Assembly* on September 25, 2015. This agenda is a comprehensive action plan designed to benefit people, the planet, and prosperity, aiming to bolster global peace and ensure justice for all. It is structured around five key pillars: planet, people, prosperity, peace, and partnerships, collectively known as the 5 Ps.

Spain, drawing on over 25 years of experience in support, aid, and cooperative endeavors, has played an active role in shaping this global framework, particularly in defining the seventeen Sustainable Development Goals (SDGs):[90]

1. End poverty in all its forms everywhere.
2. End hunger, achieve food security and improved nutrition, and promote sustainable agriculture.
3. Ensure healthy lives and promote well-being for all at all ages.
4. Ensure inclusive and equitable quality education and promote lifelong learning opportunities for all.
5. Achieve gender equality and empower all women and girls.

---

[89] Ministry of Labor, Migration, and Social Security. (n.d.). http://www.mitramiss.gob.es/redretos/es/presentacion/index.htm
[90] United Nations. (n.d.). *Sustainable Development Goals.* https://www.un.org/sustainabledevelopment/es/objetivos-de-desarrollo-sostenible/

6. Ensure availability and sustainable management of water and sanitation for all.
7. Ensure access to affordable, reliable, sustainable, and modern energy for all.
8. Promote sustained, inclusive, sustainable economic growth, full and productive employment, and decent work.
9. Build resilient infrastructure, promote inclusive and sustainable industrialization, and foster innovation.
10. Reduce inequality within and among countries.
11. Make cities and human settlements inclusive, safe, resilient, and sustainable.
12. Ensure sustainable consumption and production patterns.
13. Take urgent action to combat climate change and its impacts*.
14. Conserve and sustainably use the oceans, seas, and marine resources for sustainable development.
15. Protect, restore, and promote sustainable use of terrestrial ecosystems, sustainably manage forests, combat desertification, and halt and reverse land degradation and biodiversity loss.
16. Promote peaceful and inclusive societies for sustainable development, provide access to justice for all, and build effective, accountable, and inclusive institutions at all levels.
17. Strengthen the means of implementation and revitalize the global partnership for sustainable development.

Highlighting recent initiatives in Spain, Spanish banks' notable adherence to the UN's Principles for Responsible Banking in September 2019 is a prime example. This commitment was formalized in New York, with one hundred and thirty global banks (in the financial sector) signing the declaration. These principles include:

- Strategic Alignment: The institutions pledge to synchronize their business strategies with the goals outlined in the SDGs and the Paris Agreement.
- Impact Optimization and Target Setting: There will be a commitment to enhance positive impacts while minimizing negative ones, focusing efforts on areas of most significant potential influence.
- Client Engagement: The organizations commit to responsibly engaging with their clients to foster sustainable practices and create mutual prosperity for present and future generations.
- Stakeholder Collaboration: Those who sign these principles agree to engage, consult, and collaborate actively with relevant stakeholders to fulfill societal goals.
- Governance and Corporate Culture: The institutions will establish public goals and pursue them via robust governance frameworks and a culture of responsible banking, aiming to mitigate the most detrimental effects of their operations.
- Accountability and Transparency: These principles will be subject to regular evaluations, emphasizing transparency and accepting full accountability for both positive and negative impacts.

Several initiatives have been implemented in southern Spain, specifically by the Junta de Andalucía to encourage companies to adopt socially responsible practices. Notably, the "Government Council Agreement," dated October 18, 2016, stands out for advocating the inclusion of social and environmental clauses in the contracts managed by the Autonomous Community of Andalusia. These provisions aim to fulfill social, ethical, and environmental policy goals, ensuring job creation, decent work conditions, social inclusion, equality of opportunity, work-life balance, ethical business practices, and environmental respect.

The *Sustainable Economy Fund in Andalusia*[91] champions CSR by facilitating various initiatives, including job placement efforts, bolstering environmental and social sustainability, addressing matters of equality and work-life balance through negotiations, encouraging CSR among self-employed individuals, social economy entities and entrepreneurs, advancing equality and work-life balance strategies, and endorsing best practices and environmental volunteerism.[92]

---

[91] InfoAyudas. (n.d.). FES - *Sustainable Economy Fund*. https://www.infoayudas.com/Infoayudas-FES-Fondo-de-Economia-Sostenible—64185.php

[92] The Andalusian Environmental Volunteering Program stands out as a leading European initiative in fostering public engagement in environmental conservation, sustainability, and education, as well as in rural areas' social and cultural development. Initiated in 1995 by the Ministry of the Environment and in collaboration with various social organizations, this program serves as an institutional effort to support environmental volunteer activities within the region. Since its inception, it has engaged over 45,000 Andalusians in 4,000 direct actions to protect the environment and support diverse projects. Retrieved from https://www.juntadeandalucia.es/organismos/agriculturaganaderiapesc aydesarrollosostenible/areas/educacion-informacion-ambiental/voluntariado.html

CORPORATE SOCIAL RESPONSIBILITY APPLIED TO THE COMPANIES

The European Competitiveness Report 2008[93] by the *European Commission* identifies six key indicators that connect CSR with the competitive edge of firms:

A. Cost Structure: The debate continues whether CSR significantly reduces company costs, given the impact of various direct factors (such as industry, context, and company size). However, the environmental aspect of CSR is recognized for its effect.

B. Human Resources: CSR is a tool for attracting, motivating, and retaining staff, enhancing job stability, and developing interpersonal relationships by fostering a workplace culture that embraces diversity and leverages knowledge.

C. Customer Perspective: CSR shapes a company's strategy, market positioning, and competitiveness,

---

[93] European Commission (2008). *European Competitiveness Report 2008*. thfile:///C:/Users/marti/Downloads/cr-2008-final_4058.pdf

boosting demand in markets associated with ethical trade, government procurement/sales, and supply chains of the more engaged private sector.

D. Innovation: Engaging with stakeholders through CSR fosters innovation that addresses social and environmental issues, creating value for the company. This is achieved through improved working conditions that stimulate innovative thinking.

E. Risk and Reputation Management: Implementing CSR in risk and reputation management involves assessing adherence to Human Rights and striving for maximum transparency in corporate operations.

F. Financial Performance: CSR enhances financial reporting and market transparency, establishing a positive relationship between socially responsible investing (SRI) and financial performance.

Granda (2012) outlines four essential elements required to develop a comprehensive CSR strategy within an organization: Firstly, Leadership (1) is described as the obligation of company executives to formulate strategies and manage the aspects of a responsible entity, where the governance of CSR (2) is integrated into the business's goals and values, both individually and collectively. These components should be reinforced through implementing communication and transparency measures (3) in financial reporting and showcasing effective social and environmental stewardship. Consequently, this approach fosters a dialogue with stakeholders (4), enabling the organization to assess the impact of its activities and address and mitigate future social and environmental challenges.[94] Today, the company is pivotal in reaching significant societal enhancement and

---

[94] Granda, G. (2012). Fundamentals of socially responsible management. In J.I. Galán Zazo & A. Sáenz de Miera (Eds.), *Reflections on corporate*

progress objectives.[95] Engaging in initiatives like "business in the community" and "corporate community involvement" puts forward strategies that channel its benefits back to society and foster sustained investment plans. These strategies align the company's goals with the social, environmental, and economic requirements of the community it serves.

BENEFITS OF THE APPLICATION OF CORPORATE SOCIAL RESPONSIBILITY IN COMPANIES

A primary aim for businesses is to establish themselves as exemplary *corporate citizens*. Attaining this status, the advantageous impact of CSR on employees, the environment, stakeholders, and the broader public sets them apart from competitors. Moreover, CSR-driven strategies significantly shape potential clients' perceptions and purchasing choices, allowing businesses to forge meaningful connections with their communities. The rewards of engaging in corporate social responsibility are predominantly intangible, enriching the company's reputation and relational assets.[96]

For many, the primary benefit of CSR is its unique role in enhancing a critical intangible asset for the company: its reputation. This is an extension of quality management,

social responsibility in the 21st century (pp. 165-166). Salamanca, Spain: University of Salamanca Editions.

[95] García de Oteyza, M.O. (2012). Fundamentals of socially responsible management. In J.I. Galán Zazo & A. Sáenz de Miera (Eds.), *Reflections on corporate social responsibility in the 21st century* (pp. 89-104). Salamanca, Spain: University of Salamanca.

[96] Komodromos, M., & Melanthiou, Y. (2014). Corporate reputation through strategic corporate social responsibility: Insights from service industry companies. *Journal of Promotion Management, 20*(4), 470-478.

with reputation being the outcome of effective brand management.[97] Despite the challenges in measuring reputation, its significance in bolstering the company's economic vitality is undeniable.

CSR has emerged as a crucial internal factor in organizational success in the current business environment.[98] CSR strategies enable businesses to adopt and evolve commercial activities that foster economic, social, cultural, and environmental benefits for various stakeholders. In today's landscape, where sustainability and social impact are paramount, companies with robust CSR frameworks are more attractive to investors who prioritize sustainability and ethical corporate governance. This preference is manifested through increased interest in sustainable investments and support for innovations addressing global social and environmental issues. Consequently, companies that invest in CSR strategies often achieve superior levels of quality, productivity, and competitiveness, benefiting from the commitment of their employees and stakeholders. This commitment is visible in the enhanced market value of their shares and increased trading activity. Moreover, these companies see better employee retention rates. They are more successful in attracting new talent, particularly among the younger generation, who highly value employment within organizations that demonstrate a commitment to ethical and sustainable practices.

[97] Moreno Izquierdo, J.A. (2004). Corporate social responsibility and competitiveness: A view from the company. *R.V.E.H.*, *12*(3), 9-50.
[98] Toro, O., & Rey, G. (1996). *Private company and social responsibility*. Bogotá: Impreandes.

DOMAINS OF CORPORATE SOCIAL RESPONSIBILITY WITHIN THE ORGANIZATION

CSR encompasses all aspects of a company's management, requiring a thorough examination of its activities to identify its direct and indirect impacts. According to the *Corporate Social Responsibility Observatory*,[99] this leads us to a cross-cutting idea that impacts multiple areas. There is a growing recognition of the importance of responsible governance among investors, customers, employees, and government bodies. Companies increasingly realize that adapting to changing demands involves managing new risks and presents significant opportunities. These opportunities include the development of innovative products or services and the exploration of new markets. By doing so, businesses can meet emerging needs and address society's challenges in the new millennium.[100]

The Green Book (2001) identifies two distinct aspects of corporate social responsibility:

A. The **internal dimension** focuses on ethical practices inside the organization, impacting employees, health and safety, adaptation to change, and environmental management related to using natural resources in production processes.

---

[99] Corporate Social Responsibility Observatory. (n.d.). Non-profit organization dedicated to promoting the correct application of CSR, founded in 2004 in Madrid by several civil society organizations. https://observatoriorsc.org/ambitos-de-la-rsc/#

[100] Granda, G. (2012). Fundamentals of socially responsible management. In J.I. Galán Zazo & A. Sáenz de Miera (Eds.), *Reflections on corporate social responsibility in the 21st century* (pp. 165-166). Salamanca: University of Salamanca Editions.

B. The **external dimension** involves responsibilities outside the organization, encompassing relationships with business partners, suppliers, consumers, governmental entities, and non-governmental organizations. This dimension primarily supports the rights and interests of local communities and environmental protection.

THE INTERNAL DIMENSION OF THE COMPANY

HUMAN RESOURCES

Several vital principles underpin human resources management within organizations: individuals are distinct, each with unique backgrounds and a rich array of knowledge, skills, and abilities crucial for the effective management and strategic activation of organizational resources. As vital components of the organization, they provide invaluable intelligence, creativity, and learning capacity, essential for its ongoing innovation and competitiveness in a constantly evolving landscape of challenges and changes. They serve as dynamic contributors and possess critical competencies necessary for the organization's success against its competitors, pivotal in guiding the organization toward excellence and achievement. People, viewed as human capital within the organization, represent a significant asset contributing intelligence to its operations.[101] Consequently, contemporary approaches to human resource management emphasize the need for organizations to invest in the training and development of their leaders, including managers and directors. These leaders embody the organization's commitment to fostering social responsibility, contributing

---

[101] Chiavenato, I. (2009). *Human talent management* (3rd ed.). Mexico: McGraw-Hill.

to sustainable human development through their dedication and trust towards its employees, their families, and the wider society.

When implementing CSR within human resources, companies must focus on several key areas: fostering free collective bargaining, ensuring gender equality, eliminating discrimination based on age, ethnicity, race, religion, or disability, and supporting work-life balance. Additionally, developing and disseminating a code of conduct for management is crucial, with regular updates and checks to ensure adherence. Moreover, companies must prioritize the prevention of occupational hazards and safeguarding health and safety at work while also focusing on enhancing the profitability, quality, and efficiency of their operations.[102] Regarding gender equality, the *World Economic Forum's* "Gender Gap Report 2023"[103] underscores the necessity of enacting more impactful policies to realize gender parity in the workplace. This includes strategies such as ensuring transparency in pay and enhancing the representation of women in leadership roles.

Among the four typologies of business culture, one is characterized by adaptability, highlighting organizations that embed policies and values designed to recognize, understand, and react to evolving environmental signals.[104] This adaptive culture prizes creativity, willingness to take

[102] Fuentes García, F.J., Veroz Herradón, R., & Saco De Larriva, F. (2006). Social responsibility in human resource management. In L. Vargas Escudero (Coord.), *Myths and realities of corporate social responsibility in Spain: A multidisciplinary approach* (pp. 137-178). Navarra, Spain: Thomson Civitas.

[103] World Economic Forum. (n.d.). *Global Gender Gap Report 2023.* https://www.weforum.org/publications/global-gender-gap-report-2023/

[104] Daft, R. (2005). *Administration* (6th ed.). Mexico: Thomson.

risks, and empowerment.[105] As noted in the *Harvard Business Review's* "Business and Sustainability Report 2023,"[106] the difficulties brought on by the COVID-19 pandemic and climate change challenges have evidenced the necessity for business cultures that are both more adaptable and resilient. This underlines the critical role of agility and sustainable innovation within organizations.

STRUCTURE

The framework for CSR, outlined by the *Spanish Association of Accounting and Business Administration* (AECA) in 2004, describes socially responsible investment as the most prominent form of endorsing corporate social responsibility within financial markets. This investment approach prioritizes ethical, environmental, and social considerations alongside financial factors in the decision-making process, defining the "responsible shareholder." These shareholders seek adequate investment returns and demand transparency and accuracy in companies' financial and social disclosures. Additionally, they expect integrity and accountability from the management team, which plays a crucial role in garnering the confidence of potential investors and ensuring the company's longevity.

The AECA (2009) posits that, over time, CSR has emerged as a critical indicator of an organization's future financial performance and a magnet for long-term investments. This aligns with the principles of the *Spanish Strategy for Corporate*

---

[105] Empowerment refers to a management strategy utilized by the human resources departments of many companies to improve outcomes. This approach involves granting employees autonomy, responsibility, and authority to address issues and make decisions without needing approval from higher-ups.
[106] Harvard Office for Sustainability. (n.d.). https://sustainable.harvard.edu/data-and-sustainability-progress/2022-annual-report

Social Responsibility (EERSE) (2014), which advocates for CSR as a catalyst for responsible and sustainable growth. According to the EERSE, there's a pressing need to educate financial analysts and investors on the significance of incorporating sustainability criteria into their decision-making processes. This approach should become a fundamental business standard and a key to maintaining competitiveness. Socially responsible investing directs capital towards more sustainable activities and industries, prioritizing the financing of the real economy over speculative ventures and adopting a long-term outlook.

Reports from the ESG Commission and *KPMG Trends*[107] for the 2023 agenda and Forética's insights into ESG trends shaping the sustainability agenda in 2023[108] highlight the growing prominence of socially responsible investing. This trend is marked by a notable rise in engagement from younger investors and an increased emphasis on initiatives related to renewable energy.

PROCESSES

In shaping the internal CSR framework for the marble industry, the final aspect involves refining the companies' internal processes. According to the *Junta de Andalucía*'s 2007 "Guide to Internal Social Responsibility and Human Resources," these processes originate from an intangible realm akin to interpersonal relationships. They focus on fostering a conducive atmosphere within organizations. This strategy

---

[107] KPMG Trends. (2023). ESG commission: The sustainability control tower. https://www.tendencias.kpmg.es/2023/04/comision-esg-torre-control-sostenibilidad/

[108] DIRCOMFIDENCIAL. (2023). ESG trends that will mark the sustainability agenda in 2023. https://dircomfidencial.com/rsc/tendencias-esg-qu e-marcaran-la-agenda-de-sostenibilidad-en-2023-20230130-1427/

draws from three key areas: the modern understanding of organizational ecology, the integration of professional, personal, and family life, and the implementation of environmental initiatives to enhance the internal corporate environment. Such measures are designed to improve the workplace and extend their positive impact on the broader ecological and community well-being.

Furthermore, this Guide expands on organizational ecology, viewing it as a societal expectation that pushes businesses to extend their influence beyond their internal boundaries to address human impacts on climate and the natural environment. This perspective transcends the goal of maintaining a positive internal organizational climate, urging employees and companies to engage in eco-efficiency, environmental stewardship, and conservation of natural resources. This is framed not just as a corporate responsibility but as a critical matter for the survival of humanity itself.

Environmental responsibility has driven the expansion of internal corporate social responsibility (CSR) into domains like ecology and the implementation of socially beneficial environmental improvements that impact society. This evolution reflects the heightened awareness and responsiveness that internal CSR requires from businesses,[109] integrating contemporary insights within organizational ecology and CSR frameworks. The United Nations' "Report on the Sustainable Development Goals 2023: Special Edition"[110]

---

[109] European Commission. (n.d.). *Green Book*. https://eur-lex.europa.eu/legal-content/ES/TXT/PDF/?uri=CELEX:52004DC0334

[110] United Nations. (2023). Report on the Sustainable Development Goals: Special Edition 2023. https://mexico.un.org/es/239254-informe-sobre-los-objetivos-de-desarrollo-sostenible-2023-edici%C3%B3n-especial

and the *Spanish Ministry for the Ecological Transition*'s "First Report on Ecological Transition in the Recovery, Transformation, and Resilience Plan"[111] underscore the critical role of adopting sustainable practices and green technologies in corporate strategies. The UN report emphasizes the imperative of actions to address climate change and foster equality. In contrast, the Spanish report details the country's initiatives in advancing ecological transition, highlighting investments in renewable and energy-efficient technologies. These developments point to an increasing commitment to sustainability and carbon footprint reduction, aligning with the Sustainable Development Goals within the scope of corporate social responsibility.

In this analysis, the focus on managing environmental impact and natural resources begins as an element of internal CSR despite its effects that blur the lines between a company's internal and external environments. This approach is informed by the linkage of such management practices to the principles of eco-efficiency and sustainability, leading to environmental responsibilities that extend beyond company policies to involve all employees as collective stakeholders.

The *European Commission's Green Paper* further highlights the importance of regulating atmospheric emissions and maintaining a respectful engagement with the natural world. This shared responsibility encompasses the entire marble industry, including the corporate entities and their professionals, emphasizing a conscious commitment and

---

[111] Ministry for the Ecological Transition and the Demographic Challenge. (2023). *The MITECO publishes the first report on ecological transition in the Recovery, Transformation, and Resilience Plan.* https://www.miteco.gob.es/es/prensa/ultimas-noticias/2023/12/miteco-p ublica-primer-informe-transicion-ecologica-en-recovery-plan-transformation-and-resilience.html

the practical implications for the sustainable use of natural resources. This theme will be explored in greater depth in later sections dedicated to examining CSR practices within the marble sector.

THE EXTERNAL DIMENSION OF THE COMPANY

SOCIAL AND CULTURAL ENVIRONMENT

A business can positively impact its community and broader society by employing local workers, bolstering the region's economic growth, or through philanthropy. Initiatives aimed at directly benefiting the immediate neighborhood are also accessible to small enterprises since they don't necessarily require additional financial outlays but instead rely on allocating human resources.[112]

CSR initiatives can also benefit society by donating products or services, engaging employees in volunteer efforts, helping vulnerable individuals find jobs, and financially supporting projects. While some of these activities may require more significant investment, they can be adapted for implementation by a wide range of organizations. Furthermore, private companies can play a pivotal role in supporting community development by aligning their efforts with public policies, especially in sectors like the marble industry, where they wield significant technological and economic influence. By collaborating not just through financial donations but also by leveraging their technological expertise, managerial skills, marketing capabilities, and other

---

[112] Lafuente, A., Viñuales, V., Pueyo, R., & Llaría, J. (2003). *Corporate social responsibility and public policies*. Madrid: Ecology and Development Foundation.

resources, businesses can significantly contribute to societal advancement.[113]

Considering intellectual property as part of CSR initiatives is crucial within the cultural sector. The advantages of incorporating CSR and investing in culture extend beyond enhancing a company's reputation, visibility, and brand image. They also foster customer loyalty by embedding the company within the local community's cultural fabric and collective identity. This engagement yields a tangible positive impact, elevating cultural responsibility strategies above mere marketing, advertising, and sponsorship efforts. Consequently, a responsible marble company should actively participate in its community's social and cultural life. It contributes to economic prosperity and should also shape and enrich its local environment, promoting mutual growth.[114]

ENVIRONMENT

The external ecological dimension is one of the six critical aspects of corporate social responsibility, highlighting organizations' efforts to protect the environment. This encompasses all actions taken to conserve the environment, irrespective of the resources utilized, the pollution level, and the organization's geographic location. Every activity involved in producing goods or providing services has an environmental impact. Such activities disrupt the equilibrium

---

[113] Kliksberg, B. (2012). The crisis and corporate social responsibility. In J.I. Galán & A. Sáenz de Miera (Eds.), *Reflections on corporate social responsibility in the 21st century* (p. 61). Salamanca: University of Salamanca.

[114] Ruiz, D. (2012, November 28). Corporate social responsibility and investment in culture: An approximation. *Economy and Culture*. https://economiaycultura.wordpress.com/2012/11/28/responsibilidad-social-corporativa-e-inversion-en-cultura-una-aproximacion/

of ecosystems, leading to numerous environmental changes, collectively called environmental impacts.[115]

Companies' environmental impact can be beneficial or detrimental depending on their operational practices, influencing their financial outcomes due to potential environmental damages. This consideration is crucial for devising medium—and long-term production strategies and processes. Hence, it is imperative for marble companies, among others, to seek out technologies, programs, strategies, and policies that minimize environmental degradation and sustain their economic and financial viability by optimizing resource utilization, including the reuse of byproducts or waste from their production activities.

Mitigating the adverse environmental effects necessitates a comprehensive approach that encompasses the prevention and reduction of environmental impacts at their source to facilitate corrective actions, the monitoring and regulation of impact factors and their ecological consequences, the preliminary assessment of potential environmental impacts and risks associated with project undertakings, and the pursuit of research aimed at resolving specific issues and enhancing environmental stewardship.[116]

Advancements in technology, including digitalization, artificial intelligence, and renewable energy sources, are becoming increasingly critical in diminishing businesses' environmental footprints. Integrating these technologies has the potential to notably lower carbon emissions and enhance

---

[115] CSR Action. (2007). *Guide for the environmentally responsible company.* Santiago de Chile: CSR Action.
[116] CSR Action. (2007). *Guide for the environmentally responsible company.* Santiago de Chile: CSR Action

resource efficiency.[117] Moreover, the emphasis on supply chain sustainability is gaining prominence. Businesses are extending their environmental responsibility beyond their immediate operations to include the ecological impact of their suppliers and partners.[118]

THE ROLE OF CORPORATE SOCIAL RESPONSIBILITY (CSR) IN ENHANCING A COMPANY'S VISIBILITY THROUGH COMPREHENSIVE COMMUNICATION

Comprehensive communication within organizations represents a novel approach to understanding, studying, and managing communication, applicable to various entities, including foundations, commercial businesses, service providers, non-profits, public agencies, and government bodies. This modern perspective integrates different domains and professionals involved in organizational communication, encouraging them to work together synergistically and cohesively. By leveraging everyone's skills, competencies, and roles, the aim is to align various communication efforts under a unified strategic framework.[119] In today's communication landscape for businesses, it is crucial to focus on managing "intangible assets" such as reputation, image, branding, knowledge, and corporate social responsibility. These

---

[117] Sivaram, V., & Kann, S. (2020). Renewable energy and AI: Harnessing the power of the sun. *Nature*. https://www.nature.com/nature/volumes/585

[118] Kate Mc Loughlin, K. Lewis, D. Lascelles, & S. Nudurupati. (2023). Sustainability in supply chains: Reevaluating business process management, *Production*

Planning & Control, 34(1), 19-52. DOI:10.1080/09537287.2021.1884764

[119] Rivero Hernández, M. (2017). *Principles of comprehensive communication in organizations*. Cancun, Mexico: La Salle University.

elements are vital for adding value to the organization, serving as foundational pillars that enhance offerings and increase appeal.[120]

Communicating a company's values and strengths, including those in the marble industry, is often most effectively achieved through initiatives managed by the public relations sector. Regular dissemination of Corporate Social Responsibility (CSR) initiatives as part of an organization's communication strategy can significantly enhance its reputation across media outlets, digital platforms, social networks, and public institutions.

However, it's crucial to distinguish between CSR communications and the company's advertising or promotional content. The overuse of CSR as a marketing tool in media has led to skepticism among journalists, who argue that companies should finance this content due to its promotional nature. The misuse of social programs as the cornerstone of CSR strategies has been noted.[121] The ethical considerations in advertising should guide the crafting and dissemination of messages across traditional and digital mediums.[122] For numerous businesses, adherence to these ethical standards is a measure for implementing CSR tools to bolster their image.

[120] Carrillo Durán, M.V., Núñez de Prado Clavell, S., Tato Jiménez, J.L., Delgado Pérez, J.P., Carrillo, M.V., Tato, J.L., & García, M. (2013). The panorama of comprehensive communication policies and CSR management in Mexican SMEs. *Intangible Capital, 9*(1), 20-45.

[121] Andreu Pinillos, A., & Fernández Fernández, J.L. (2011). From CSR to corporate sustainability: A necessary evolution for value creation. *Harvard-Deusto Business Reviews, 207*, 5-21.

[122] Castelló Martínez, A. (2012). Advertising saturation in new digital environments: An ethical question? In J.C. Suárez Villegas (Ed.), *Communication ethics at the beginning of the 21st century: First international conference on communication ethics, book of minutes* (pp. 1128-1138). Seville: Faculty of Communication of the University of Seville.

This approach requires consistency in what companies claim to be, their actions, and their communications, coupled with a commitment to transparency and engagement.[123]

To foster a proper balance between responsibility, publicity, and trust, a company should adhere to three guiding principles:[124] first, articulate and publicly commit to a comprehensive CSR framework formulated and refined through discussions with relevant stakeholders, grounded in ethical principles. Second, identify the stakeholder groups associated with the company, understand their interests, and outline methods of dialogue, communication, and transparency that facilitate the participation of all affected parties. Third, ensure that these principles are continuously reviewed and updated to reflect evolving societal expectations and company practices.

CSR serves as a strategic tool within the marketing arsenal. When combined with legal accountability and business ethics, a company can enhance its functional and symbolic reputation, showcasing its tangible and intangible qualities and shaping consumer perceptions.[125] By communicating CSR efforts promptly, coherently, and consistently, a company can significantly improve its standing among stakeholders. This improvement is crucial for cultivating consumer loyalty and achieving a favorable market position.[126]

[123] Pérez Chavarría, M. (2009). Corporate social responsibility (CSR) and communication: The agenda of large Mexican companies. *Sign and Thought, 28*(55), 201-217.

[124] García Marzá, D. (2006). Business ethics: A framework for the definition and management of CSR. In L. Vargas Escudero (Coord.), *Myths and realities of CSR in Spain. A multidisciplinary approach.* Navarra, Spain: Aranzadi.

[125] He, Y., & Keung Lai, K. (2014). The effect of corporate social responsibility on brand loyalty: The mediating role of brand image. *Total Quality Management & Business Excellence, 25*(3-4), 249-263.

[126] Vega Muñoz, P. (2012). Corporate social responsibility (CSR) as a strategic communication instrument to increase brand value:

It's important to emphasize the "cohesive" strategic importance of CSR for the "internal customer." Evidence suggests that a worker who is content with their job represents an invaluable asset for a company offering a competitive edge. The prosperity of contemporary organizations increasingly depends on their ability to engage employees in their business ventures, ensuring that all staff members align their personal goals with the company's objectives.[127]

CORPORATE SOCIAL RESPONSIBILITY WITHIN THE REALM OF HOLISTIC ONLINE COMMUNICATION

In today's era, the digital transformation and technological advancement of business operations have become evident, affecting both the organizational structures and the processes that shape how professionals interact with stakeholders and clients. The contemporary societal landscape calls for bidirectional communication between clients and users, a demand facilitated by the internet: We are entering a new phase of communication within a burgeoning digital society that necessitates innovative communication methods.[128] Modern digital formats offer platforms for interactive dialogue between companies and

---

The case of television advertising. [Master's thesis, Universidad Andina Simón Bolívar, Ecuador]. Institutional Repository UASB. http://repositorio.uasb.edu.ec/bitstream/10644/2955/1/T1048-MC-Vega-La%20responsabilidad

[127] López-Guzmán Guzmán, T.J., Sánchez Cañizares, S.M., & Nascimento Jesús, M.M. (2010). Job satisfaction as an intangible value of human resources: A case study in hotel establishments. *Theory and Praxis*, 7, 35-53.

[128] Cabezuelo Lorenzo, F. (2013). Five years of crisis in the communication market (2008-2013). *History and Social Communication*, 18, 713-725.

consumers, presenting a more cost-effective alternative to traditional one-way advertising.

Despite previous discussions, the marble industry still has significant progress to make. It's crucial to note that over five years ago, the deployment of websites was fundamental for sharing information about a company's CSR initiatives. However, in Spain, the corporate websites of the Spanish IBEX 35 companies of that era lacked interactivity, with most CSR communication being one-directional: "On their corporate websites, companies were at an elementary stage of utilizing the web, primarily for information dissemination rather than engaging and dialoguing with the audience."[129] This gap was more pronounced considering that internet users were already becoming more environmentally conscious and technologically savvy at the dawn of the new millennium.[130] While not directly business-related, this trend has a solid connection to CSR strategies implemented by companies, as environmental awareness among both companies and users reinforces brand values. Therefore, companies must recognize the need to professionally tailor their business communication and advertising strategies to the nuances of 2.0 platforms. Doing so can maximize the platforms' potential for virality, customer orientation, public engagement, loyalty, and brand building.[131]

---

[129] Moreno, A., & Capriotti, P. (2006). The communication of Spanish companies on their corporate websites: Analysis of social responsibility, corporate citizenship, and sustainable development information. *Zer: Journal of Communication Studies, 11*(21), 47-62.

[130] Castelló Martínez, A. (2010). Environmental awareness in online social networks: Introduction to advertising media research. *Magazine of the Ibero-American Forum on Communication Strategies, 13*, 23-47.

[131] Ros Diego, V.J., & Castelló Martínez, A. (2011). Communicating responsibility on social media. *Latin Journal of Social Communication, 67*, 47-67.

Over a decade since those initial insights, the landscape of Web 2.0, characterized by information evolving into interactive communication among users, has been significantly advanced. This progression first moved through Web 3.0, which integrates human knowledge with artificial intelligence via content optimization to forge neural networks. It then evolved into Web 4.0, a stage where various forms of intelligence converge globally across all available tools and devices. Web 4.0 represents a digital revolution that defines the current era, aiming to digitalize the production process with minimal human or manual input. Its goal is to encompass a broad spectrum of industries and to refine and enhance current technologies. This advancement seeks to meet the demands of digital manufacturing more fully, illustrating a leap toward a future where digital integration is paramount. The advancement of the web has led to the emergence of an algorithm-driven society, marked by the simultaneous generation of vast amounts of data (big data), which plays a pivotal role in shaping the fourth industrial revolution. This shift signifies a crucial move towards creating an intelligent and sustainable industrial landscape, with big data analysis at its core.[132] We are transitioning towards a fifth generation, presenting an even more significant challenge for businesses.

The discussions up to this point underscore the essential nature of digital tools and platforms, including corporate websites and social media, in the CSR communication strategies of marble companies. This new virtual and digital landscape fosters a more dynamic and interactive

[132] Sharma, A., & Kumar Jain, D. (2020). Industry development 4.0. In A. Nayyar & A. Kumar (Eds.), *A roadmap to industry 4.0: Smart production, sustainable business, and sustainable development* (pp. 57-72). Cham, Switzerland: Springer Nature Switzerland.

relationship between companies, the public, and stakeholders. It enables the creation of connections highlighting the socially responsible initiatives undertaken by companies, thus enhancing their corporate credibility.[133]

STAKEHOLDER ENGAGEMENT IN COMPREHENSIVE CORPORATE SOCIAL RESPONSIBILITY COMMUNICATION

As times have evolved with cultural, political, and social shifts, marble companies have understood that their role extends beyond wealth generation's 'simple' aim. They recognize the existence of an inextricable bidirectional relationship with their surrounding environment. Consequently, the methods and mediums a company employs for communication (including the channels, formats, and target audiences) significantly shape its culture, image, and corporate reputation. Whether deliberately managed or not, all actions and communications from the company establish a connection with its environment.[134]

This realization underscores the importance of identifying and managing the relationships between the company and its key stakeholder groups, recognizing the responsibilities and benefits of these relationships. The primary stakeholders in the context of CSR include shareholders and investors,

[133] Valdiviezo Abad, K.C., & Agila Cambizaca, M.A. (2017). Social networks as an instrument for disseminating social responsibility in the communication areas of the business sector. In F.J. Herrero Gutiérrez & C. Mateos Martín (Eds.), *From the verb to the bit* (pp. 1729-1753). La Laguna, Tenerife: University of La Laguna. http://www.revistalatinacs.org/16SLCS/libro-colectivo-edicion-2.html
[134] Orjuela Córdoba, S. (2011). Communication in the management of corporate social responsibility. *Correspondences & Analysis, 1,* 138-156.

customers, suppliers, employees, regulatory bodies, and the broader society.[135]

- **Shareholders and Investors:** The company is responsible for ensuring sound management, economic returns, clear communication, transparency, and ethical investing for its shareholders and investors. The primary benefits of nurturing a strong relationship with this group include mitigating, or at least reducing, conflicts and disruptions and fostering an environment conducive to increased investments.

- **Customers:** The company's obligation to customers revolves around meeting expectations and efficiently establishing and maintaining communication channels. Properly managing customer relations yields significant benefits, such as enhancing their perception of the company's transparency and averting negative campaigns, potential complaints, and litigation.

- **Suppliers:** The company must avoid power misuse by fostering communication mechanisms that enhance interaction and align mutual interests with suppliers. Effective strategies with suppliers lead to several key advantages, including a broader selection power and productivity and service quality improvements.

- **Employees:** The company upholds its employees' fundamental human and labor rights. This involves setting up structures and processes that emphasize comprehensive communication and training. The key benefits of effectively managing this responsibility include fostering a sense of employee pride and belonging, retaining talent, and enhancing productivity.

---

[135] Azuero, D. (2009). *CSR communication: Proposals for a responsible communication model*. Madrid: Forética.

- **Regulatory Institutions:** The company's duty towards regulatory bodies involves devising and executing a plan for communication and transparency and undertaking initiatives that support national development and environmental respect. This approach has primary advantages, including fostering a sense of identification between the company and citizens, increasing collaborative efforts, and improving relationships between institutions.
- **Society:** The company is directly responsible to the society within which it operates. It must develop and implement various channels, strategies, and plans for communication and transparency that promote local development in an environmentally friendly manner. The main benefit of a stronger relationship with society is the emotional connection that forms between the company and community groups, enhancing the company's reputation and support within the community.

The feedback companies receive from their stakeholders should reflect the transmission of values deemed constructive by these groups that align with the company's institutional identity. Digitalization and online platforms have revolutionized this interaction, enabling more direct and tailored communication via social networks and online forums. The significance of CSR to these stakeholders hinges on legal, ethical, and philanthropic considerations, with sustainability and climate change becoming increasingly prominent in CSR discourse.[136] Transparency and accountability, particularly in disclosing CSR and sustainability information, are qualities that stakeholders are increasingly seeking. The impact of

---

[136] Golob, U., Lah, M., & Jancic, Z. (2008). Value orientations and consumer expectations of corporate social responsibility. *Journal of Marketing Communications*, 14(2), 83-96.

CSR initiatives, as perceived by their audiences, is inherently linked to the nature of these proposals themselves:

- The **"prosumer"** is a consumer who also becomes an information producer and product expert by sharing their insights on social networks, virtual communities, or digital forums.
- The **"crosumer"** represents a prospective buyer who seeks out the experiences of others online before committing to a well-known product, driven by skepticism towards excessive advertising. It is noted that "user-generated product information instills 80% confidence in consumers."
- The **"persumer"** concept companies should embrace, focusing on "perceiving the consumer as an individual and tailoring the product to them through interaction, aiming to comprehend their needs and modify the product accordingly to meet those needs."[137]

Despite consumers' varied and intricate characteristics on a broad scale, in the context of CSR, the "responsible consumer" is defined as one who considers the ethical practices of the companies from which they purchase. Meanwhile, the "activist consumer" initiates campaigns against companies perceived as socially irresponsible.[138]

This discussion on stakeholder engagement with CSR highlights that companies represent a network of relation-

[137] Lacruz Rengel, R. (2015). Finished objective, interface, and service: Three ontological paradigms for understanding industrial design. *DeSigno. Refereed Design Magazine of the University of Los Andes, 1*, 7-22.
[138] Vargas Niello, J. (2006). Corporate social responsibility (CSR) from the perspective of consumers. *Project Documents, 109*. Ecuador: United Nations Economic Commission for Latin America and the Caribbean (ECLAC).

ships among various parties. This underscores the connection between stakeholder theory and CSR, especially regarding CSR initiatives integral to a company's primary operations. Additionally, it suggests that other forms of CSR become essential when companies are viewed as the final recourse for addressing specific societal issues.[139]

[139] Dmytrieyev, S.D., Feedmanb, E., Hörischc, J., & Madison, J. (2021). The relationship between stakeholder theory and corporate social responsibility: Differences, similarities, and implications for social issues in management. *Journal of Management Studies.* https://doi.org/10.1111/joms.12684

CORPORATE SOCIAL RESPONSIBILITY APPLIED TO THE MARBLE COMPANY

The final years of the 2010s marked a significant shift towards overcoming the global economic downturn from 2008 to 2018. The "International Trade and Innovation in the Dimension Stone Sector"[140] report highlighted that in 2017, the global trade of stone materials reached 88.15 million tons, valued at 23.5 billion euros, with the price per ton averaging 267 euros. This represented a 14% increase in the volume of exports compared to 2016, alongside relatively stable values (with a slight increase of 1.6%), leading to a decrease in the average price per ton in 2017, as detailed in Table 2.

The XXXII World Marble and Stones Report 2021[141] noted a marked downturn in the global trade of stone in 2020, with an estimated 8% decline from the year before, translating

---

[140] Stone Sector. (2018). *Trade and innovation.* https://www.stone-ideas.com/63375/imm-carraras-stone-sector-2018/
[141] World Marble and Stones Report. (2021). *XX XXXII World Marble and Stones Report 2021.* https://www.worldstonereport.com/

to a reduction of about four million tons. This downturn was mainly due to the adverse effects of the COVID-19 pandemic on both demand and the supply chain.

Despite these obstacles, the stone industry showed remarkable resilience, mitigating much of the pandemic's negative impact. A slight decrease of 2% in global stone production was observed in 2020, with production levels reaching around 318 million tons. This performance highlights the industry's capability to adjust to shifts in market dynamics and emphasizes the significance of corporate social responsibility during such difficult periods.

Table 2. International Trade of Natural Stone

Years	Values		
	Value (millons €)	Quantity (millions t)	AUV* (euro per-ton)
2011	18821	95.4	197.35
2012	21472	96.1	223.44
2013	22437	80	280.46
2014	22857	85.9	266.08
2015	25650	75.21	341.04
2016	23928	77.34	309.39
2017	23548	88.15	267.12
2018	24,443	87.00	280.94
2019	25,373	85.86	295.48
2019	26,339	84.73	310.77

Processing: IMM.nb;* AUV: average unit value of the traded materials (imports and exports).

Source: XXXII World Marble and Stones Report 2021.

On the global stage, the *World Trade Atlas* (2018) identified China as the leading exporter of ornamental stones despite a decrease in its market share from 40% in 2016 to 34.4% in 2017. Regarding the demand for international stone products, China's imports reached 2.4 billion euros in 2017, outperforming the United States by over 167 million euros. Italy secured the position as the second-largest market share holder with 13.8% of the global market, followed by Turkey (13.5%), India (11.2%), Brazil (6.9%), and Spain (3.6%).

By 2020, the XXXII World Marble and Stones Report 2021 highlighted an uptick in Asia's contribution to worldwide production, claiming over 66% of the total, a significant portion of which was attributed to China, India, and Turkey, leading the global mining industry. Despite hitting a plateau in exports, China ramped up its domestic production to meet local demand, showcasing an adaptive strategy distinct from other major Asian producers who remain export-oriented. The collective output of China, India, and Turkey accounted for nearly 60% of the global total, marking an increase of about three percentage points from the previous year and achieving a new record high. [Tabla3]

Table 3. World stonework production and theoretical performance for the year 2020

ZonEs	tons	%	Mill. eq. sq. mt. / cm^2 - Total	Waste	Net
EU/28	19,000	12.3	352	144	208
OTHERS EUROPE	2,500	1.6	46	19	28
EUROPE	21,500	13.9	398	163	235

ZonEs	tons	%	Mill. eq. sq. mt. / cm^2 – Total	Waste	Net
NORTH AMERICA	5,250	3.4	96	39	57
LATIN AMERICA	12,250	7.9	226	93	133
AMERICA	17,500	11.3	322	132	190
CHINA	52,500	33.9	972	398	574
INDIA	27,500	17.7	508	208	300
TURKEY	11,250	7.3	208	86	122
OTHERS ASIA	14,250	9.2	264	108	156
ASIA	105,500	68.1	1,952	800	1,152
AFRICA	10,000	6.4	185	76	109
OCEANIA	500	0.3	10	4	6
WORLD	155,000	100.0	2,865	1,175	1,690

Source: XXXII World Marble and Stones Report 2021.

On the other hand, Brazil and Iran kept their production levels steady, each approaching eight million tons. Italy, ranked sixth, experienced a reduction in production due to declining exports and a stagnant domestic construction sector, leading to its global market share falling to 3.4%, a noticeable decrease from 17.7% two and a half decades ago. This downturn was similarly observed in Spain, Portugal, and Greece, underscoring a critical condition that had developed over the years but now had more pronounced consequences than trends seen in the United States. [Table 4]. This situation shows the industry's challenges and emphasizes the importance of adopting corporate social responsibility strategies to lessen the economic fallout and foster sustainability.

Table 4: Largest world productions

COUNTRIES	2015	%	2016	%	2017	%	2018	%	2019	%	2020	%
CHINA	45000	32.1	46000	31.7	49000	32.2	48000	31.4	50000	32.4	52500	33.9
INDIA	21000	15.0	23500	16.2	24500	16.1	26000	17.0	26500	17.2	27500	17.7
TURKEY	10500	7.5	10750	7.4	12250	8.1	12000	7.8	11750	7.6	11250	7.3
BRAZIL	8200	5.9	8500	5.9	8350	5.5	8250	5.4	8200	5.3	8000	5.2
IRAN	7500	5.4	8000	5.5	8700	5.7	9000	5.9	8250	5.3	7800	5.
italy	6500	4.6	6250	4.3	6300	4.1	6000	3.9	5850	3.8	5250	3.4
EGYPT	5000	3.5	5250	3.6	5300	3.5	5000	3.3	5000	3.2	5000	3.2
SPAIN	4750	3.4	5000	3.4	4900	3.2	4950	3.2	4850	3.1	4500	2.9
USA	2700	1.9	2800	1.9	2750	1.8	2850	1.9	3150	2.0	3200	2.1
PORTUGAL	2700	1.9	2600	1.8	2750	1.8	3000	2.0	3350	2.2	2850	1.8
PAKISTAN	1050	0.7	1100	0.7	1100	0.7	1200	0.7	1250	0.8	1300	0.8
S. ARABIA	1200	0.9	1250	0.9	1250	0.8	1300	0.8	1250	0.8	1250	0.8
GREECE	1250	0.9	1200	0.8	1500	1.0	1450	1.0	1400	0.9	1200	0.8
FRANCE	1250	0.9	1300	0.9	1350	0.9	1350	0.9	1200	0.8	1150	0.7
SUB-TOTAL	118600	84.3	123500	85.0	130000	85.4	130350	85.2	132000	85.4	132750	85.6
OTHERS	21400	15.7	21500	15.0	22000	14.6	22650	14.8	22000	14.4	22250	35.4
WORLD	46500	100	140000	100	152000	100	153000	100	154500	100	155000	100

Source: XXXII World Marble and Stones Report 2021.

The natural stone market has seen impressive growth, especially in Asia/Pacific, mirroring broader economic and industrial developments. The market's value surge, from 23.5 billion euros in 2017 to 32.4 billion euros (approximately 348 billion dollars) in 2023, signifies a rebound from the 2008-2018 financial downturn and the sector's rapid growth and transformation.

In Spain, assessing the impact of these developments and global trends on the mineral market after the economic downturn necessitates a detailed examination of the marble industry. This analysis should consider historical and current perspectives of the country's extractive economic activities. The 2021 stone cluster report shows that the industry has undergone considerable modifications across its entire production chain, from extraction to sales and distribution. Despite challenges heightened by the economic recession and the COVID-19 pandemic, the industry's output climbed to 1.7 billion euros in 2021, marking a 6.25% increase from the previous year. Furthermore, exports saw a 12% rise in the same period [table 5].

Table 5: Natural stone exports by CNAE (2021)

CNAE	2019 (milllons €)	2020 (millions €)	2021 (millions €)	% Increase 2021/20
2370	582	571	658	15,24%
0811	246	244	256	4,92%
Total	828	815	914	12,15%

Source: Clúster Piedra 2021.

A more pertinent examination, if achievable, involves the recovery and revitalization of a business infrastructure severely impacted by a decade-long widespread crisis from 2008 to 2018,[142] notably affecting the construction industry and other economic activities connected to it through the infamous "real estate bubble." During this period, the individualistic approach adopted by owners and managers of Spanish marble companies, prioritizing personal gain over the collective benefit of the extraction industry, resulted in an economic strategy characterized by cut-throat competition. This was an attempt to solidify their market foothold, inadvertently leading to a price war that significantly weakened portions of the industry amidst the financial turmoil.[143] The raw marble sector, encompassing factories and quarries, bore the brunt of these conflicts. The culmination of these strategies discredited the industry, pointing towards enhancing the mineral product as the sole viable strategy to reverse these adverse trends.

---

[142] This study designates this specific time frame because, according to the Living Conditions Survey (ECV) released by the National Institute of Statistics (INE), the average income per person in 2017 increased to 11,412 euros, marking a 3.1% rise from the previous year. This figure surpassed the 2008 average income of 11,318 euros for the first time, the year the economic crisis began, indicating a significant turning point for household financial difficulties. However, when looking at the average income per household, it hasn't yet returned to its peak levels. In 2017, it was recorded at 28,417 euros, below the 2008 figure of over 30,000 euros, albeit it showed progress from 27,558 euros in 2016. Nonetheless, matching the 2008 income levels does not equate to regaining the same purchasing power, as inflation from that year up to 2017 increased living costs by 11.4%.

The Gini index, a measure of income and wealth distribution inequality within a country, ranges between 0 (absolute equality) and 100 (absolute inequality). Spain's Gini index in 2017 was 33.2, nearly a point decrease from 34.1 the previous year, yet still 0.3 points higher than in 2008.

[143] Abad Coloma, R. (2017-2018). *The marble sector in the Vinalopó area: Analysis of the last decades and its economic, social, territorial, and landscape impacts* [Final degree project, University of Alicante]. UA Institutional Repository. http://rua.ua.es/dspace/handle/10045/76728

During the economic downturn, the marble industry witnessed a decline in its business network and workforce, paralleling a fall in production. This downturn was somewhat anticipated, given that after a period of stable growth in 2005 and 2006; there was a minor reduction in production in 2007, which became more pronounced in 2008, with earnings dropping to 2,503 million euros from the previous year's 3,202.39 million euros. However, by 2021, the industry saw a recovery, with revenues reaching 1,700 million euros, marking a 6.25% increase from 2020. In 2019, revenues were at 1,594 million euros, maintaining the same level as in 2018.[144] The years between 2017 and 2019 were critical in charting a path out of the 2008 economic crisis, with national mining production escalating to 3,280 million euros in 2017,[145] a 13% increase from the previous year (falling to 3,339 million euros in 2019, a 4% decrease from 2018). Looking at the last five years, the total production value has marginally surpassed the figure reached in 2013 (3,254 million euros). Between 2017 and 2021, Spain ranked as the seventh-largest global producer and the sixth-largest exporter of minerals (natural stone), resulting in a significantly positive trade balance for the country's natural stone sector.[146]

While the figures might appear promising, the Spanish marble sector has faced concerning shifts in the distribution of subsector contributions to its overall value, particularly leading up to the onset of the global health crisis caused by COVID-19 in early 2020. Notably, the share of ornamental rocks[147] in the

---

[144] Clúster Piedra. (2019). *Sector report 2021*. https://clusterpiedra.com/wp-content/uploads/2022/04/Informe-sectorial-CLUSTER-PIE-DRA-2021.pdf

[145] Millions of euros.

[146] Ministry of Ecological Transition. (2017, 2019). *Mining Statistics Report of Spain*. Retrieved from https://www.statista.com/statistics/425726/production-value-mining-quarrying-sector-spain/

[147] Ornamental rocks include alabaster, sandstone, limestone, quartzite, granite, marble, and slate. This report excludes quarry products such

sector's total value has remained relatively stable compared to other subsectors despite experiencing a production decline of about 37% from 2005 to 2017.[148] Between 2017 and 2019, ornamental rock production fluctuated between €394 million and €374 million, with marble accounting for 11% of the total annual production value. This trend highlights a significant downturn in the sector, especially considering that ornamental rock production was valued at €440 million at the start of the last decade, with marble contributing 14% to the overall value.

While direct employment in the Spanish mining sector from 2013 to 2017 remained steady, showing a gradual and continuous recovery from 2014 onwards, a negative trend emerges when considering the employment-to-number of operations ratios. In 2017 and 2019, out of 2,759 and 2,665 mining operations, ornamental rocks accounted for 18% and 17% of the production activities, respectively. Regarding the size of these operations in terms of employment, they con- stituted 28% and 28.6%, respectively, of the total sector employment in the country. Among these companies, three-quarters employed between one to nine workers, with 85% and 76% of their staff primarily fitting within this employee range.[149]

The Stone Cluster reports from 2016, 2019, and 2021 highlight a notable trend: the sector has seen a significantly higher rate of closures among companies focused on extraction than those involved in production. This pattern arises because extraction

---

as limestone, sand and gravel, gypsum, granite, siliceous sand, clay, marl, crete, and dolomite from its consideration.

[148] Ministry of Ecological Transition. (2005, 2010, 2015). *Mining Statistics Report of Spain*.

[149] Mining Statistics Report of Spain. (2017, 2019). Published by the Ministry of Ecological Transition.

firms typically possess larger asset volumes to sustain and exhibit less adaptability in response to drops in revenue. Despite this, the job losses within processing companies are also substantial, with these businesses undergoing downsizing as a near-desperate measure to fend off shutdowns.

The mining industry, which produces mineral materials for commercial purposes, is strategically situated across the country's geography.[150] These industries are predominantly found in inland regions with limited resources and rely heavily on a singular economic activity. Characterized by the size of the enterprises, the majority are small and medium-sized businesses (SMEs) with a pronounced family influence and a modest number of employees, particularly those involved with natural stone. These companies operate quarries with significant potential and depend on the support industry for the technical and material resources necessary for their operations. This potential has facilitated their growth and expansion over the past decade. An essential component of this industrial framework includes retail businesses, often called "marblers," that cater to the natural stone processing indus- try. These retailers are crucial, bringing together thousands of micro and small-sized companies in their operations.

While ornamental rock extraction occurs across most of Spain's seventeen autonomous communities, Galicia, the Valencian Community, and Andalusia collectively account for 70% of the country's total production value. The Valencian Community and Galicia lead in sales, with Castilla y León, Murcia, and others trailing significantly behind, as reported by Clúster Piedra in 2021. In Andalusia, 830 companies in

[150] Piedra Cluster. (2016, 2019, 2021). Sector report. https://clusterpie- dra.com/wp-content/uploads/2022/04/Informe-sectorial-CLUS- TER-PIEDRA-2021.pdf

2018 were extracting and processing ornamental rocks.[151] Specifically, in the province of Almería, 287 firms are based, with 227 (or 79.09%) situated in the Almanzora region and 213 in the "Marble Region," a sub-region dependent on it.[152] [153]

Through the lens of Corporate Social Responsibility (CSR), the stone industry has demonstrated remarkable resilience amid economic adversities and the global health crisis. Despite facing immediate hurdles, including a downturn in production and workforce numbers in 2020, the XXXII World Marble and Stones Report 2021 anticipates a gradual resurgence starting in late 2021. By 2025, the sector is expected to see a significant uptick in stone supply and demand, heralding a robust recovery and sustaining an upward growth trajectory over the long haul.

The international landscape of the stone sector reveals stark variances in trade performance across different nations, with some experiencing nearly exponential growth while others contend with substantial declines. The capacity for adaptation and the strategic approaches employed have been crucial to these outcomes. Notably, countries like Turkey,

---

[151] CNAE codes include 0811 (Extraction of ornamental and building stones, limestone, gypsum, chalk, and slate), 0990 (Support activities for other mining and quarrying), and 2370 (Cutting, shaping, and finishing of stone).

[152] The marble region, encompassing Macael, Olula del Río, Purchena, Fines, and Cantoria, forms a subset of the Almanzora region, which includes Albox, Alcóntar, Arboleas, Bacares, Cantoria, Chercos, Fines, Laroya, Líjar, Lúcar, Macael, Olula del Río, Oria, Partaloa, Purchena, Serón, Sierro, Suflí, Taberno, Tíjola, Urrácal, and Zurgena. Key areas within the marble region are Macael, Olula del Río, Fines, Cantoria, and Purchena.

[153] SABI is a specialized database offering comprehensive details on companies within Spain and Portugal. The Mining Panorama Report 2017 was compiled by the Geological and Mining Institute of Spain (IGME).

India, China, and, to a lesser degree, Brazil and Greece have shown impressive growth in their stone sectors.

Many influences, including domestic demand, construction activities, demographic trends, national income levels, and environmental and mining regulations, have shaped the stone sector's trajectory. Over time, a general trend towards growth has emerged, particularly in Asia, which has led in both production and consumption. Nonetheless, trend shifts are always possible, underscoring the need for support from institutional and supranational bodies, especially within established economies.

Looking to the medium term, the prospects for the stone sector appear cautiously optimistic. While various constraints may temper global growth, the sector and its affiliated industries are in a solid position to perpetuate their historical upward trend. This progress is expected to make a meaningful contribution to economic, social, and infrastructural development, bolstering confidence in a world in greater need than ever.

CORPORATE SOCIAL RESPONSIBILITY IN SMALL, MEDIUM, AND LARGE COMPANIES (SMES) IN THE MARBLE SECTOR

Actions and plans for corporate social responsibility (CSR) in small and medium-sized enterprises (SMEs) remain underdeveloped, impacting their economic growth.[154]

---

[154] Hean Lee, M., Ka Mak, A., & Pang, A. (2012). Bridging the gap: An exploratory study of corporate social responsibility among SMEs in Singapore. *Journal of Public Relations Research, 24*(4), 299-317.

The sustainable business governance code suggests that CSR strategy in SMEs should encompass three holistic aspects:[155] strategic thinking, action, and communication, with sustainability as the core principle. This approach ensures that CSR is effectively integrated into all facets of the business, promoting a balance between economic, social, and environmental objectives.

The owner's role in small and medium-sized enterprises (SMEs) is crucial. They often embody the organization's leadership and direction. They play a vital role in embedding corporate social responsibility (CSR) by leading by example and engaging daily with stakeholders such as suppliers, customers, employees, competitors, and the community. This approach ensures that CSR becomes ingrained in SMEs, making it essential for these businesses to have the necessary tools to support its implementation effectively.

CSR represents a forward-thinking and secure investment, capable of generating profits and ensuring long-term business prosperity. SMEs, especially those in the marble industry, must recognize their environmental responsibilities and community engagements, showcasing their contributions to the market. It's not about inventing new practices but enhancing existing ones with social or environmental value. This approach demonstrates environmental responsibility while fostering national and economic growth, a perspective SMEs must adopt and adapt to ensure their future success and sustainability.[156]

---

[155] Based on the Good Practices Guide (2011) introduced by the Impulsa RSE-SME project of the Ministry of Industry, Tourism, and Commerce of the Government of Spain.

[156] Medrano Sánchez, M.I., Masías Vidal, J.L., Obeso Cuadra, J.K., Morón Paredes, G., Moreano Márquez, W.L., García Segovia, M.E., & Coveñas Lalupu, J. (2019). Corporate social responsibility in the relationship

While it's acknowledged that larger entities predominantly advance CSR practices in the marble industry due to SMEs claiming insufficient resources, this stance is viewed not as a valid excuse but as a challenge to overcome. The emphasis is on reframing the lack of resources from a deterrent to a motivator for implementing CSR strategies, encouraging a shift in perspective among smaller companies.

During this period of recovery and rebuilding post-COVID-19, it is crucial for SMEs in the marble industry to unite and champion CSR implementation, fostering partnerships to explore collective solutions. SMEs must engage with their local communities, ensuring that mining operations and social lives progress sustainably and harmoniously. Emphasizing local development not only supports community well-being but also strengthens the economic foundations of these businesses.

In the context of the challenges of the COVID-19 pandemic, Raimo et al. (2021)[157] explore the proactive engagement of Spanish firms with society. Their study of fourteen Madrid Stock Exchange-listed companies reveals a collaborative effort with NGOs to offer crucial support, focusing on food, health, and social aid for those most in need. This research underlines the critical role of CSR in crisis response, showcasing its effectiveness in aiding community recovery and strengthening, thereby emphasizing the value of corporate-community partnerships during times of adversity.

---

between peasant communities and mining companies. *Lex Faculty of Law and Political Sciences of the Alas Peruanas University*, 17(23), 327-360.

[157] Raimo, N., Rella, A., Vitolla, F., Sánchez-Vicente, M. I., & García-Sánchez, I. (2021). Corporate social responsibility in the COVID-19 pandemic period: A traditional way to address new social issues.

While CSR poses challenges for SMEs, it offers mining multinationals strategic opportunities to broaden their client base and market reach, acting as a unique form of engagement. Moreover, it is a competitive edge, with companies adopting CSR strategies gaining advantages like enhanced customer loyalty, improved brand reputation, and stronger connections with public and private entities. This approach benefits companies operationally and contributes to their standing as responsible corporate citizens.[158]

INITIATIVES AND SCOPE OF CORPORATE SOCIAL RESPONSIBILITY IN THE MARBLE INDUSTRY

Mining activities lead to environmental and socio-economic changes, altering landscapes, livelihoods, and local economies from pre- and post-extraction phases. Within ethical and sustainable management contexts, the mining sector's economic impact has drawn significant attention from various stakeholders. Mining companies are now confronted with the necessity to navigate the complexities of modern sustainability challenges.[159]

Corporate social responsibility (CSR) in the marble sector should extend beyond company philanthropy to embrace sustainable development within the industry's ecosystem over the next decade.[160] Sustainability is the cornerstone for achieving social and economic equilibrium by enacting

[158] Peña Gutiérrez, D. (2011). *Research, documentation, and reporting on the impacts of Spanish multinationals in Latin America*. Bolivia: Observatory of Multinationals in Latin America (OMAL).

[159] Törey, S. (2004). The mining company: From the target of criticism to the pioneering action. *Environment and Development, 20,* 78-81.

[160] Arias Arce, V., Lovera Dávila, D., Puente Santibañez, L., & Calderón Celis, M. (2009). Context of mining social responsibility and governance. *Journal of the FIGMMG Research Institute, 12*(23), 60-67.

measures that pave the way for a shared future.[161] CSR aims for sustainable economic advancement amidst socioeconomic disparities and environmentally detrimental practices. With environmental stewardship becoming integral to strategic planning, organizations strive to mitigate their adverse impacts. Achieving a sustainable balance necessitates more than government action; it requires a corporate commitment to fulfill its pivotal role in supporting all stakeholders.

Despite the previous discussion on the social and economic benefits of sustainability for marble companies, the shortcomings and insufficient implementation of corporate social responsibility initiatives among Spanish SMEs are a significant contemporary issue. While there is a growing recognition of their strategic importance for the medium and long term—evident on many companies' websites, where themes of sustainability, safety, health, sports, education, and societal engagement are highlighted—the principal declarations currently tend to be confined to general statements somewhat related to sustainability.

HUMAN RESOURCES

One of the key global trends[162] shaping the future of sustainable governance is the focus on human rights within global supply chains.[163] The interconnected nature of international commerce has spotlighted supply chains as conduits linking developed economies to various human rights abuses. Large

[161] Aguilera Castro, A., & Puerto Becerra, D.P. (2012). Business growth based on social responsibility. *Scientific Journal Thought and Management, 32*, 1-26.

[162] Global Agenda 2030. (n.d.). Retrieved from https://www.agenda2030.gob.es/es/objetivos

[163] FORÉTICA. (2018). *FORÉTICA 2018 Report: On the evolution of CSR and Sustainability - The optimist's reward.* https://bibliotecadigital.ccb.org.co/items/73ed1806-b151-498f-9789-c69a69c2e7a4

corporations, wielding influence sometimes surpassing that of states, are increasingly recognized as pivotal in advancing the human rights agenda. Consequently, enhancing product traceability for human rights compliance has become essential to corporate due diligence, underscoring businesses' vital role in promoting ethical practices.

As the economy becomes more digitalized, green employment is increasingly prominent. Green jobs, aimed at enhancing environmental quality, boosting energy efficiency, and minimizing carbon footprints, are becoming vital for sustainability and corporate social responsibility. These positions play a crucial role in environmental conservation and offer avenues for professional growth and adaptation in the evolving job market.

The advent of digitalization—including big data, artificial intelligence, robotization, and automation—will lead to the displacement of many jobs while simultaneously creating new, currently unimaginable roles. This shift will sharpen diversity policies and their impact on employee health and well-being, making them more integral to corporate social responsibility agendas in the coming years.

Corporate social responsibility is a vital link between organizations, their employees, their families, and the community, fostering a work environment of harmony and peace. For marble companies, the critical challenges include recruiting skilled workers and ensuring their retention through continuous training and development, enhancing internal communication, balancing work-life dynamics, embracing diversity, providing equitable pay and career opportunities, especially for women, and incorporating safety and professional development as core organizational values. These efforts aim to create a workplace that values inclusivity and employee well-being.[164]

Despite efforts by governmental and academic entities, the marble industry continues to grapple with significant human rights challenges for its workers. Issues like low wages, extended work hours, and the failure to compensate for actual hours worked severely impact work-life balance, disproportionately affecting women. Additionally, workplace safety and health concerns are prominent,[165] particularly for those in high-risk roles within this sector known for its hazardous conditions and elevated accident rates, occasionally resulting in fatalities.

In Spain, the emphasis on worker safety and health, especially within the marble industry, has notably increased, evidenced by legal and regulatory efforts to safeguard against work-related risks. The adoption of the ISO 45001[166] standard, superseding OHSAS 18001, exemplifies the industry's commitment to enhancing occupational health and safety practices through systematic management. This standard prioritizes risk control, worker involvement, and leadership engagement, aiming to integrate proactive safety measures within existing management systems for improved workplace safety initiatives.

The Government of Andalusia has embarked on developing the Strategy for Sustainable Mining, setting a direction for the

---

[164] Medrano Sánchez, M.I., Masías Vidal, J.L., Obeso Cuadra, J.K., Morón Paredes, G., Moreano Márquez, W.L., García Segovia, M.E., & Coveñas Lalupu, J. (2019). Corporate social responsibility in the relationship between peasant communities and mining companies. *Lex Faculty of Law and Political Science of the Universidad Alas Peruanas*, 17(23), 327-360.

[165] López Trujillo, N. (2016, June 5). Exploited women speak "like Chinese" in Elche. *El Español*. https://www.elespanol.com/reportajes/201606 04/129987157_0.html

[166] ISO 45001. Occupational health and safety management systems.

sector's regional policy through 2030. This forward-looking strategy aims to enhance the entire mining industry's value chain, elevate competitiveness, encourage global business expansion, foster research into mineral resources, and ensure long-term environmental sustainability and safety practices. It represents a significant update from the 2020 strategy, marking a comprehensive approach to supporting sustainable growth and internationalization of the Andalusian mining sector. The strategic framework emphasizes fostering job creation and enhancing the mining sector's competitiveness through multiple human capital initiatives: an annual mining safety inspection plan, occupational risk incentives, SME and self-employed subsidies for risk prevention projects, action programs for high-accident-rate companies, and comprehensive training for government officials and the business community to improve employability. Concurrently, the Safety Inspection Plan, managed by the Directorate of Labor Relations and Occupational Health and Safety, aims to ensure mining operations adhere to safety regulations, facilitating a comprehensive understanding of all mining-related accidents and incidents.

In Andalusia, there's a proactive approach towards fostering workplace safety through subsidy programs for SMEs and the self-employed, exemplified by the PAEMSA initiative targeting companies with high accident rates to bolster their preventive efforts. Additionally, the region has launched a comprehensive Shock Plan against Workplace Accidents, building on the extended Safety and Health at Work Strategy 2017-2022 (extended until 2023).[167] This includes creating an Accident Rate Map and enhancing company audits and

---

[167] Junta de Andalucía. (n.d.). Andalusian Occupational Health and Safety Strategy 2017-2022, extended to 2023. https://www.juntadeandalucia.es/sites/default/files/2022-07/EASST_2017_2022_complete.pdf

information efforts, thereby augmenting and broadening the scope of the PAEMSA's objectives.

Andalusia's initiatives, particularly notable for its large number of marble companies, showcase strategic efforts to enhance the Spanish mining sector's capabilities amidst new challenges. These efforts include continuous training programs for educators and technical staff on new technologies, legal-administrative frameworks, and organizational changes, focusing on addressing female unemployment. Furthermore, vocational training opportunities, scholarship availability, and real-world internships in extractive industries provide a robust foundation for boosting student employability post-graduation, demonstrating a comprehensive approach to workforce development in regions impacted by mining activities.

THE STATUS OF WOMEN AND YOUNG PEOPLE

Spain's Marble Schools emphasize employability and job access in the natural stone sector, highlighting the importance of vocational training. Collaboration with public employment services and the Ministry of Education and Vocational Training is becoming a norm in the natural stone professional field. These partnerships focus on delivering targeted training, especially to unemployed people, vulnerable groups, and workers in the natural stone industry, to support and develop the sector's skills base.

Similarly, specialized technological centers in the marble industry coordinate activities for women at risk of exclusion, youths, and individuals over 45, alongside Vocational Training centers, instructors, and industry entrepreneurs. The primary goal is to foster women's integration into the stone sector, where they remain underrepresented across the industry's value chain. Despite the natural stone sector's global market leadership and the modern application of stone, women's participation is minimal due to gender integration issues, with a feminization rate of only 7.25% in Europe.[168] Pilar Martínez-Cosentino Alfonso, Vice President of Grupo Cosentino, emphasizes enhancing women's leadership positions within the marble industry, advocating for increased female prominence and meritocracy.[169]

Gender discrimination in the marble market and industry is a clear issue, reflecting a broader societal challenge. The pursuit of work-life balance often leads to women scaling back or leaving their careers due to inflexible working conditions. This approach hinders the attainment of genuine gender equality by perpetuating a system where short-term fixes fail to address the root cause of gender disparity.

Since March 2020, the onset of the COVID-19 pandemic and the subsequent state of emergency declared by the Spanish government have underscored the need for strategic corporate adjustments. During this prolonged period of health, social, and economic turmoil, public and private businesses have been compelled to adapt their strategies. Echoing lessons from the 2008 crisis, Professor Gayle Allard from IE University points out the importance of protecting employees as a core element of corporate social responsibility (CSR). By avoiding layoffs and adopting flexible work arrangements, companies can retain skilled workers and foster loyalty, benefiting all

---

[168] Clúster Piedra. (2016). Sector report 2016. https://clusterpiedra. com/2018/01/informe-sectorial-cluster-piedra-2016/

[169] Statements made to the Ibero-American communication company Corresponsables. https://www.corresponsables.com/entrevistas/ods5-pilar-martinez-cosentino-alfonso-mujeres-puestos-directivos-meritocracia-top-100-mujeres-espana-liderazgo-femenino

parties involved, particularly young people and women, when normalcy returns.[170]

ENVIRONMENT

The journal "Social Responsibility in Mining" highlights the crucial link between mining operations and their social and environmental impact, advocating for socially responsible actions. The magazine underscores that mining projects with higher social acceptance enjoy better long-term sustainability. It positions corporate social responsibility at the forefront, emphasizing the need to balance mining activities with social well-being and environmental preservation. This approach is essential for achieving long-term success and acceptance in the mining sector. This concept is relevant to Spain, where the rampant use of natural resources and the subsequent rise in waste from developmental activities necessitate implementing more efficient management and production systems. Such systems aim to foster a sustainable developmental process, highlighting the need for strategies that ensure environmental sustainability alongside economic growth.[171]

Marble mining and associated activities significantly impact the environment, leading to landscape changes and industrial waste. Recognizing these impacts, both public and private sectors have initiated measures like quarry reconstruction, relocating businesses to reduce urban noise, and regulating waste disposal. The primary motivation for companies addressing waste issues is compliance with legal

---

[170] Statements made by Gayle Allard to the newspaper El País on March 21, 2020. https://elpais.com/economia/negocio/2020-03-20/la-hora-de-la-verdad-para-el-nuevo-capitalismo.html

[171] Santos, A., Villegas, N., & Betancourt, J. (2012). Marble waste as an input in civil construction: Diagnosis of the Lagunera Region. *Construction Magazine, 12*(22), 17-26.

requirements, with a vast majority (90.4%) acknowledging this as their main reason for action.[172]

The 2004 report "References for quality and eco-efficiency in the construction sector in Murcia"[173] identifies key environmental impacts from construction activities, including dust, vibrations, and noise; landscape changes; water usage; and the production of wastewater and waste. This highlights the sector's broad ecological footprint, underscoring the need for sustainable practices.

Dust and vibration emissions significantly impact the environment. They originate from explosions in large rock quarries that fracture the rock to extract materials. Additionally, these vibrations are constantly present in large primary crushing and screening facilities, affecting all company personnel at various levels.

While quarry noises are intermittent and stem from specific activities such as blasting, they also arise from daily operations like engine starts, material loading into dump trucks, and more. Moreover, specific noise emissions are continuously generated by loading machinery, dust collectors, or conveyor belts at extraction sites, contributing to overall noise pollution.

The report highlights that mineral extraction significantly impacts the landscape's aesthetic and visual aspects, as such operations cover extensive areas. It emphasizes the

---

[172] Cajamar Foundation. (2010). Value Reporting Foundation, Integrated Reporting: https://integratedreporting.org/
[173] Ministry of Agriculture, Water and Environment of the Region of Murcia. (2004). *References for environmental quality and eco-efficiency in the construction sector in Murcia*. Baetica S.L. https://dspace.carm.es/jspui/bitstream/20.500.11914/2892/1/ReferentesSectorConstruccion.pdf

detrimental effects on water quality due to the need for water and direct discharges into rivers. Furthermore, the alteration to the landscape caused by mining activities depends on the local topography, type of landscape, and the area's existing flora and fauna. In rock extraction, two types of materials are produced: organic soils and rugged, rocky substrates, which are not immediately usable by the mining operation/exploitation itself.

Non-valuable by-products, such as inert waste and 'bargains' -*gangas*- emerge throughout production. Additionally, the water treatment process in washing and cutting operations often produces 'fines' and sludge. This waste, especially sludge, poses a significant environmental challenge by contaminating the water table and adjacent lands, highlighting a need for improved waste management practices to mitigate environmental impact.

The portion of the original rock that can be used ranges from 30 to 70 percent. The remaining material, including lower-quality rocks, layers lacking ornamental value, and waste from cutting, is repurposed in the construction industry to create artificial blocks, aggregates, and industrial minerals. If not reused, these materials are often disposed of in landfills.

The report emphasizes that quarry operations can disrupt original habitats, necessitating landscape restoration projects to revive pre-exploitation conditions as closely as possible. Eco-efficient strategies from successful cases focus on reducing water use and mitigating environmental impacts, notably through reusing inert waste and rehabilitating land affected by mining activities.

Marble quarrying has an efficiency of only about 20%, leading to 80% of the extracted material being waste. This waste, largely unsuitable for use except as raw material for aggregates, poses significant environmental challenges. It necessitates proper landfilling to manage its disposal, impacting surrounding land and water sources. A strategy to mitigate this waste issue involves its temporary storage in landfills for future recycling and utilization, aiming to minimize the environmental footprint of marble quarry operations.

Implementing a waste recovery system in the marble industry offers significant technological and environmental benefits. Notably, it enables the recuperation and reduction of marble waste produced during extraction and processing. The waste is transformed into products of various sizes suitable for public construction projects, enhancing resource efficiency and reducing environmental impact by employing wet crushing techniques.

Spain's Ministry for the Ecological Transition issued guidelines in 2019[174] for rehabilitating abandoned mining waste facilities, aligning with Royal Decree 975/2009. This decree, aimed at managing mining waste and rehabilitating affected areas, reflects significant updates in technical aspects and compliance with the EU Directive 2006/21/EC. This approach emphasizes environmental protection in mining activities, waste management, and restoring impacted landscapes.

The guide clarifies Royal Decree 975/2009's usage of "rehabilitation" over the traditional term "restoration" for accuracy. Rehabilitation focuses on treating land

---

[174] Guide for the rehabilitation of abandoned mining waste facilities. https://cpage.mpr.gob.es/producto/guia-para-la-rehabilitacion-de-insta-laciones-abandonadas-de-residuos-mineros/

impacted by mining to ensure its return to a satisfactory state. This encompasses improving soil quality, restoring fauna and natural habitats, freshwater systems, and landscapes, and providing land that can be used beneficially, aligning with Directive 2006/21/EC's objectives for comprehensive environmental recovery post-mining activities. These regulations recognize that the terms restoration and rehabilitation can be used interchangeably. Mining operators and marble workers must rehabilitate the natural areas affected by their operations, including disposal sites for mining waste, using their resources. They must submit a Restoration Plan to the mining authority outlining how they will comply with the environmental restoration requirements stipulated in R.D. 975/2009.

Recognizing the crucial role of mining in Andalusia's social and economic fabric, the regional government approved the Andalusian Mineral Resources Management Plan (PORMIAN) through a decree on June 28, 2016. This plan, aligning with the Andalusian Mining Strategy 2020, serves as a strategic framework for guiding research and the extraction of mineral resources across Andalusia, emphasizing thoughtful planning and management to maximize benefits and mitigate impacts. The PORMIAN aims notably to ensure that mining activities are environmentally integrated and compatible with other economic activities based on exploiting different territorial resources. It mandates quarry operators to secure administrative authorization before commencing operations, especially for quarries in public or forestry domains. Additionally, it requires operators to provide financial guarantees[175] for proper execution, ensuring responsible management and minimization of environmental impacts

---

[175] Focuspiedra. (n.d.). A new plan for the management of mining waste will allow the definition of guarantees in Macael. https://www.

within Andalusia's diverse territorial resources. (Centro Tecnológico Andaluz de la piedra, 2013)

FROM WASTE TO RESOURCES

The "Applied Soil Science" research group from the University of Almería, alongside collaborators from the University of Granada, Polytechnic of Murcia, and Leitat Technological Center in Barcelona, have pioneered a method for repurposing marble sludge to rehabilitate areas contaminated with heavy metals. Their work facilitates vegetation growth, enhancing environmental restoration and reducing visual pollution. The University of Alicante's team has innovated in sustainable marble waste applications through the REMISACO[176] project, utilizing marble by-products (*marmolina*) in civil engineering, significantly offsetting the industry's landfill contributions. The REMISACO project stands out for its environmental impact by offering a solution for the approximately 125,000 tonnes of marble waste sent to landfills annually. This initiative marks a significant advancement in sustainable waste management within the marble industry, showcasing an innovative approach to repurposing industrial by-products.

Building on the momentum of innovation and sustainability, the Polytechnic University of Valencia and the University of Granada have explored the utilization of marble waste in creating new types of eco-friendly concrete. This waste serves dual roles as an aggregate and an active ingredient enhancing concrete's properties. Such research underscores a leap forward in sustainable industrial waste management

focuspiedra.com/un-nuevo-plan-de-gestion-de-residuos-mineros-permitira-definir-los-avales-en-macael/

[176] Technical Environmental Magazine (RETEMA). (n.d.). New sustainable applications for marble waste. https://www.retema.es/actualidad/nuevas-aplicaciones-sostenibles-para-los-residuos-de-marmol

practices, presenting viable alternatives for recycling and reducing environmental footprints.

The Andalusian Government's Department of Innovation, Science, and Business spearheads initiatives to repurpose marble cutting and polishing waste into an asset for restoring degraded ecosystems. An expert team is tackling mine and marble waste challenges utilizing mud's unique properties. They're transforming sludge into a resource that not only neutralizes mine waste acidity and contamination but also aids in the rejuvenation of marble waste dumps. This approach leverages marble waste to fill quarry voids, promoting the growth of vegetation and enhancing the landscape's appearance.

Following the application of recovery techniques across several marble quarry slopes, there's been a notable resurgence of vegetation. This revival, triggered by sludge cover enhancing soil moisture, facilitates plant rooting. This positive outcome is evidenced in areas like the Macael and Aznalcóllar mountains in Seville, which suffered a toxic spill involving substances including copper, zinc, cadmium, arsenic, and lead nearly two decades ago, demonstrating the potential for environmental restoration even in previously contaminated landscapes.[177]

The current approach to managing mining waste emphasizes its remediation, reuse, and repurposing.[178] *Technosoil* is introduced as a viable solution, reusing waste from both

---

[177] The entire process is discussed in the study on using marble sludge and phytoextraction for remediating metal(loid) polluted soils, which is published in the *Journal of Geochemical Exploration*.

[178] Carretero Gómez, A., & Velasco Muñoz, J. F. (2018). Endogenous mining resources and territorial development: The case of the Marble Region (Almería, Spain). *Journal of Regional Studies, 111*, 51-75.

industry and agriculture in the western Almería region. This method transforms such waste into materials suitable for revitalizing degraded soils and rehabilitating waste dumps. Creating *technosoil* involves mixing 70% industrial waste, including sludge and by-products, with 25% compost from agricultural greenhouse waste and 5% bentonite, a versatile clay, to produce a functional artificial soil.[179]

Recovery practices extend to various regions in Spain, as highlighted by the Murcia Region's Marble, Stone, and Materials Technological Center (CTMARMOL). The CTMARMOL Business Research Association, supported by Spain's Biodiversity Foundation and the Ministry for the Ecological Transition, participates in projects under the 2018 climate change adaptation initiative. The Coral3D project, aligned with the National Plan for Adaptation to Climate Change, integrates 3D printing technologies and utilizes marble sector waste in coral restoration efforts, demonstrating innovative approaches to climate change adaptation in critical marine ecosystems.

These instances demonstrate that despite the significant waste produced by marble mining, viable strategies exist for its treatment and management. These approaches successfully marry economic efficiency with the environmental imperatives of sustainability, showcasing innovative solutions that repurpose waste while addressing sustainability concerns.[180]

---

[179] Cosentino S.A. (n.d.). The management of marble and agricultural waste produces technosols. https://www.aenverde.es/la-gesti on-de-residuos-del-marmol-y-de-la-agricultura-produce-los -tecnosuelos/

[180] Aznar Sánchez, J.A., García Gómez, J.J., Velasco Muñoz, J.F., & Carretero Gómez, A. (2018). Mining waste and its sustainable management: Advances in worldwide research. *Minerals, 8*, 284. https://doi.org/10.3390/min8070284

CORPORATE SOCIAL RESPONSIBILITY IN THE MARBLE SECTOR FROM THE ECONOMIC AND COVID-19 CRISIS (2008-2020) TO THE POST-CRISIS ERA

The marble sector navigates future challenges, including sustainable development, CSR initiatives beyond environmental legal compliance, human capital, and community engagement. These aspects are crucial as they align with societal expectations and demands, indicating a shift towards a more integrated approach in addressing environmental, social, and economic responsibilities.[181] These elements meet societal expectations and demands. Adopting self-regulatory mechanisms is a critical step towards managing CSR systematically, aiming for its full integration into corporations. This approach creates synergies between CSR, environmental management, occupational health and safety, and the quality of products and services. The implementation of these disciplines through systems like ISO 14001 (environmental management), ISO 45001 (occupational health and safety), and ISO 9001 (quality) has become increasingly vital in mining companies over the past two decades.

CSR initiatives in the marble industry must consider projects' social and environmental impacts, as these significantly influence local community expectations and project-related decision-making.[182] Local shareholders, deeply integrated

---

[181] Vintró Sánchez, C., & Comajuncosa Casabella, J. (2009). Corporate social responsibility in mining: Sustainable mining, 835-849. https://upcommons.upc.edu/bitstream/handle/2117/6975/Responsibilidad%20social.pdf

[182] Vintró Sánchez, C., & Comajuncosa Casabella, J. (2009). Corporate social responsibility in mining: Sustainable mining, 835-849.

into the community through their businesses, play a crucial role in economic and social advancement, moving away from a macro business model like Walmart's.[183] This shift fosters resilience between companies and their communities, highlighting the importance of local engagement and sustainable practices for long-term success and harmony between businesses and their surrounding environments.[184]

The International Council on Mining and Metals (ICMM)[185] emphasizes that economic success should not come at the expense of people or the planet, advocating for sustainable mining as a strategic advantage. Since 2003, ICMM has introduced ten fundamental principles[186] for sustainable development, focusing on applying these principles and adding eight position statements[187] on critical issues. Notably, in Spain's marble industry, the management of water resources and the transparency of mineral revenues are highlighted areas of concern. In April 2018, the International Council on Mining and Metals addressed challenges in applying its sustainability principles by broadening its focus to include various sustainability issues, aiming to bolster

---

https://upcommons.upc.edu/bitstream/handle/2117/6975/Responsibilidad%20social.pdf

[183] Walmart has been identified as the company with the highest revenue in the world, nearly half a trillion dollars annually, and as the largest private employer globally with 2.3 million employees, as reported by Forbes magazine.

[184] Kuo, S.S., & Mean, B. (2012). Corporate social responsibility after disaster. *Washington University Law Review, 89*(5), 973-1016.

[185] International Council on Mining and Metals. (n.d.). https://www.icmm.com/es

[186] The Council focuses on ethical business practices, decision-making processes, human rights, risk management, health and safety, environmental performance, biodiversity conservation, responsible production, social performance, and stakeholder engagement.

[187] Key areas of concern include climate change, tailings governance, indigenous peoples and mining, mining partnerships for development, mercury risk management, and mining in protected areas.

these mining principles. This effort focused on enhancing social and environmental standards, covering specific areas like labor rights, resettlement, gender equality, grievance mechanisms, mine closure,[188] pollution, and waste management. The adoption of these principles has been reinforced by rigorous on-site validation, ensuring credibility and promoting reporting transparency.

The marble sector is undergoing a significant transformation and is navigating outdated trends and innovative business strategies. This restructuring process involves abandoning unprofitable practices in favor of new approaches emphasizing the quality-to-price ratio, considering the raw material and its specific context. This shift aims to align the sector with current market demands and ensure its sustainability and competitiveness. Merging these approaches offers a pathway for revitalization, focusing on modernizing and adjusting the

---

[188] A quarry is recognized as a type of mine. The Ministry for the Ecological Transition and the Demographic Challenge defines mining as the industrial activity that involves the selective extraction of substances and minerals from the Earth's crust through mining techniques, potentially including explosives, to make it economically viable. Broadly, mining encompasses underground and open-pit operations and the processes involved in treating extracted mineral substances, such as crushing, sizing, washing, and concentrating, preparing them for sale and further processing. https://energia.gob.es/mineria/Paginas/Index.aspx

According to the National Institute of Safety and Health at Work (INSST) in Spain, detailed in the Encyclopedia of Health and Safety at Work published by the Ministry of Labor and Social Affairs in 2001, the primary economic goal of open-pit mines is to extract the least amount of material while achieving the maximum return on investment by processing the most marketable mineral product. The value of a vein increases with its quality. A mining plan that accurately outlines the method of extraction and treatment of the mineral is essential for minimizing capital investments and accessing the highest-value material within a vein. https://www.insst.es/documents/94886/161958/Sumario+del+Volumen+I/18ea3013-6f64-4997-88a1-0aadd719faac

entrepreneurial landscape shaped by the aftermath of the economic crisis (2008-2018), the subsequent stabilization phase (2018-beginning 2020), and the onset of the global health crisis in early 2020. This requires learning from past errors, abandoning detrimental habits, striving for a prime position in the marble market, and becoming more diverse yet specialized across various local and international levels.

The marble industry is now compelled to adopt circular economy principles, aiming for greater efficiency and profitability. This model emphasizes minimizing natural resource consumption, which often leads to environmental degradation, alongside reducing, reusing, and recycling waste. Additionally, it focuses on restoring the ecosystems and environments affected by its activities, highlighting a shift towards more sustainable and responsible production practices.

Regarding CSR, the Ministry of Finance, Industry, and Energy of the *Junta de Andalucía* emphasizes its commitment as the authority managing public mining domains. It underscores the importance of researching and exploiting mineral resources efficiently, sustainably, and safely due to their significant environmental impact. The aim is to enhance the mining sector's qualifications and safety, leveraging these valuable resources to stimulate activity and create jobs in Andalusia, ensuring a balance between economic development and environmental protection.

In 2010, the Andalusian Mineral Resources Management Plan 2010-2013 (PORMIAN) was established via Decree 369/2010 on September 7th. This plan was a strategic guide for mineral resource research and exploitation in Andalusia during the specified period. It extended the objectives of the previous

PORMIAN, with the Government Council's May 21, 2013, agreement further advancing these goals by approving the Andalusian Mining Strategy 2020, ensuring the region's continuity and evolution of mineral resource management. The June 28, 2016, agreement set forth the Andalusian Mining Strategy 2020, aimed at harnessing Andalusia's mining potential to create jobs and boost sector competitiveness. It focuses on improving mining-related public services, ensuring the sector's administrative needs are met, integrating environmental practices into mining, and promoting Andalusia's mining heritage as a multifaceted resource for sustainable development. Additionally, it seeks to foster a favorable labor relations environment, emphasizing occupational health and safety and enhancing workforce skills and job adaptability.

To align with current advancements and address contemporary challenges, the Strategy for Sustainable Mining in Andalusia 2030 (EMSA 2030)[189] was introduced and adopted on July 25, 2023. EMSA 2030 emphasizes Andalusia's mining sector's environmental, economic, and social sustainability. It aims to bolster mining as a crucial and vibrant industry and contribute to Europe's ecological and digital transition, showcasing a forward-thinking approach to sustainable mining practices.

Our focus on the Andalusian region in this book is deliberate, as Andalusia has proven its leadership in the natural stone and derivatives export market during the first quarter of 2020. Achieving record-breaking sales abroad, Andalusia commands over half of Spain's total exports in this sector

---

[189] Key topics include climate change, tailings governance, the involvement of indigenous peoples in mining, partnerships for development within the mining sector, mercury risk management, and mining in protected areas.

(55%), significantly outpacing other regions such aa the Valencian Community (14.2%) and Catalonia (13.5%), solidifying its position as a pivotal player in Spain's natural stone export industry.[190]

Continuing the upward trajectory from 2019's €624 million exports, Andalusia's natural stone and product sales in the first quarter of 2020 surged by 14% year-over-year. Almería led this growth within the region, exporting €155 million worth of goods, matching its total for all of 2019 and marking a significant 25.5% increase from 2018. This achievement set a record since the initiation of official tracking in 1995, underscoring Almería's, and more broadly Andalusia's, dominant role in Spain's natural stone market.

Over the past two years, marking the post-pandemic era and setting a precedent for future trends, Almería has continued to lead in Spain's natural stone exports. In 2022, Almería set a record with €591 million in sales during the first seven months, achieving a 27.1% increase compared to the same period in the previous year. These figures represented 99% of Andalusia's total and 59% of Spain's total natural stone exports, with a significant trade surplus of €583 million between January and July 2022. Since August 2023, Almería has sustained its leading position in exports, reaching €327 million. Until the end of 2023, Andalusia continues at the forefront of national exports, with the Valencian Community trailing at 20.3%.

---

[190] Junta de Andalucía. (n.d.). Strategy for Sustainable Mining in Andalusia 2030 (EMSA 2030). https://www.juntadeandalucia.es/organismos/transparencia/planificacion-evaluacion-estadistica/planes/detalle/435583.html

CORPORATE SOCIAL RESPONSIBILITY AS AN INTEGRATED COMMUNICATION STRATEGY IN MARBLE COMPANIES

All knowledge and truth are founded on social consensus, facilitated through communication. This process governs the acceptance or rejection of ideas, emphasizing that truth is not an inherent discovery but a collective agreement shaped through dialogue. This principle is crucial across various domains—economy, science, politics, and notably in the context of marble companies—where communication underscores the interpretation, validation, and application of facts. Consequently, consensus on knowledge or human activity necessitates robust communication channels.[191]

Understanding the dynamics of CSR communication is crucial for grasping how its meaning is established, implemented,

---

[191]   Ihlen, Ø., Bartlett, J. L., & May, S. (2011). *The handbook of communication and corporate social responsibility*. New Jersey: John Wiley & Sons, Inc.

and utilized to meet organizational goals. Communication is pivotal in commercial endeavors and CSR strategies across industries, including the marble sector. It is indispensable for reinforcing relationships with stakeholders and fostering ethical business practices. Effective communication is crucial to growth and success in the stone industry, bridging the gap between human values and the organization's created value.[192] Designing an effective CSR communication strategy involves overcoming skepticism from stakeholders while highlighting the company's socially beneficial motives.[193] By deploying communication strategies that demonstrate the alignment of social and commercial interests, a company can gain recognition for its CSR efforts. This approach enhances the company's reputation and strengthens its relationship with its audience, showing a commitment to societal welfare as integral to its business model.[194]

These communication efforts showcase a marble company's engagement in societal causes beyond its operational and commercial pursuits. In doing so, the company delineates its dedication and alignment with community-related causes by various means: financial donations, in-kind contributions, utilizing corporate assets (like marketing expertise), employee volunteerism, and applying research and development (R&D).[195] This holistic approach affirms the company's commitment to

[192] Ho Suh, Y. (2018). Business communication with corporate social responsibility. *Business Communication Research and Practice*, 1(2), 51-53.

[193] Korschun, D., Bhattacharya, C.B., & Swain, S.D. (2014). Corporate social responsibility, customer orientation, and the job performance of frontline employees. *Journal of Marketing*, 78(3), 20-37.

[194] Porter, M.E., & Kramer, M.R. (2006). Strategy & society: The link between competitive advantage and corporate social responsibility. *Harvard Business Review*, 84, 78-92.

[195] Du, S., Bhattacharya, C.B., & Sen, S. (2010). Maximizing business returns to corporate social responsibility (CSR): The role of CSR communication. *International Journal of Management Reviews*, 12, 8-19.

social responsibility and enhances its connection with the community. For SMEs in the marble industry, communication efforts must run parallel to production activities to remain competitive. Consequently, communication policies must be as strategic as corporate decisions to enhance overall outcomes. This approach ensures that SMEs can effectively convey their values, goals, and achievements, bolstering their position in the marketplace.[196]

Organizations can adopt either a marketing/commercialization model or a comprehensive communication model for their communication structures. Recently, there's been a shift towards the comprehensive/extended model, regardless of the organization's profile. This model encompasses three key areas: internal/organizational communication, institutional corporate communication, and commercial/marketing communication, aiming to create a more holistic approach to managing all aspects of organizational communication.[197] The comprehensive communication model emphasizes a unified approach, integrating all communication efforts under a singular structure and responsibility. This integration allows communication to be treated as a strategic function within the company's management. To effectively implement this model, an organization must consider all possible communication-producing areas, ensuring a cohesive and global strategy encompassing every facet of communication within the company.

[196] Carrillo Durán, M.V., Núñez de Prado Clavell, S., Tato Jiménez, J.L., Delgado Pérez, J.P., Carrillo, M.V., Tato, J.L., & García, M. (2013). The panorama of comprehensive communication policies and CSR management in Mexican SMEs. *Intangible Capital, 9*(1), 20-45.
[197] Enrique Jiménez, A.M., & Morales Serrano, F. (2010). Communication and development in the digital age. Paper presented at the AE-IC Congress, University of Malaga. https://dialnet.unirioja.es/congreso/edicion/10511

In corporate settings, the foundational theory behind comprehensive communication is acknowledging that every company's action communicates something to its audiences and stakeholders,[198] shaping its identity and personality. This model champions the strategic coordination of all forms of expression to build and enhance beneficial relationships with employees, clients, stakeholders, and the broader public. The focus isn't on the specific mix of communication disciplines employed but on ensuring these efforts collectively optimize the return on investment for the brand, facilitating constructive engagement through various mediums.

Comprehensive communication enables marble companies to integrate relationship marketing, sales promotion, and event services with traditional advertising and corporate communication. This approach aims to deliver a consistent message, uniquely positioning the company and enhancing its brand value, ensuring that all communications contribute to a coherent and distinctive brand identity. In today's context, simply being responsible isn't enough; companies must communicate their responsibility effectively.[199] Inadequate communication, characterized by information access, integrity, relevance, and accuracy issues, poses the most significant barrier to stakeholder engagement. To facilitate informed discussions on mining companies' environmental, social, and economic impacts, there's a need for collaborative research and development of sustainability indicators that

[198] Fernández, M.L. (2008). Comprehensive communication and advertising industry. *Reason and Word, 62.* http://www.razon-ypalabra.org.mx/n63/varia/madelaluz.html

[199] Palin, M. (2015). The role of CSR and CSR communication in Finnish natural stone industry [Master's thesis, Aalto University School of Business]. Institutional Repository AU. http://epub.lib.aalto.fi/en/ethesis/id/13962

can be openly shared with all interested parties, enhancing transparency and stakeholder involvement.[200]

CSR extends beyond the marble company's interaction with its environment and community, forming a core part of its management strategy. Effective communication with internal and external stakeholders is crucial, ensuring message consistency to foster trust, manage social, environmental, and economic externalities, and positively influence the extractive company's reputation. This alignment between CSR initiatives and communication strategies is vital to amplifying their impact and reinforcing the company's commitment to responsible practices.[201]

Effective communication and stakeholder management are central goals in corporate communication, and they are especially vital in the marble industry for building and safeguarding its reputation. Communication professionals can map out stakeholders by influence and interest levels, allowing for tailored communication strategies: informative, persuasive, and dialogic.[202] Identifying these strategies is critical, as it guides the choice of communication objectives across various sectors, including mining, to select the most fitting approach.

In this book section, we emphasize that communication is not merely an optional activity but an intrinsic necessity for

[200] Mutti, D., Yakovleva, N., Vazquez Brust, D., & Di Marco, M.H. (2012). Corporate social responsibility in the mining industry: Perspectives from stakeholder groups in Argentina. *Resources Policy*, 37, 212-222.

[201] Carrillo Durán, M.V., Núñez de Prado Clavell, S., Tato Jiménez, J.L., Delgado Pérez, J.P., Carrillo, M.V., Tato, J.L., & García, M. (2013). The panorama of comprehensive communication policies and CSR management in Mexican SMEs. *Intangible Capital*, 9(1), 20-45.

[202] Cornelissen, J. (2011). *Corporate communication: A guide to theory and practice* (3rd ed.). London: Sage Publications.

companies and individuals. Even in silence, organizations communicate—signaling agreement, denial, disregard, and more.[203] Thus, corporate communication should be intentionally planned and executed within a comprehensive communication framework. This entails integrating all communication plans and strategies to ensure a unified and effective approach, underscoring the fundamental role of communication in shaping perceptions and outcomes. Many marble companies have not recognized the importance of integrating communication structures and processes. The aspiration is for these companies to evolve, embracing communication through a comprehensive and cross-sectional approach. This evolution would pave the way for the professional management and planning of communication processes by experts in the field, ensuring that communication becomes a strategic pillar in their organizational framework.[204]

Incorporating CSR as a facet of corporate reputation is essential in strategic communication management. It is a tangible attribute for shaping and positioning a company's image through actions that bolster corporate reputation, creating a mutually reinforcing cycle.[205] However, marble companies must navigate this carefully, ensuring CSR communications transcend mere image and reputation enhancement. They must comprehensively address the economic, social, and environmental impacts affecting their business, providing a balanced and authentic approach to CSR.

[203] Pérez Chavarría, M. (2009). Corporate social responsibility (CSR) and communication: The agenda of large Mexican companies. *Sign and Thought, 28*(55), 201-217.

[204] Bosovsky, G. (2011). Comprehensive communication: A revolution in business thinking. *Image and Communication Magazine, 23*, 11-16.

[205] Enrique Jiménez, A.M., & Morales Serrano, F. (2010). Communication and development in the digital age. Paper presented at the AE-IC Congress, University of Malaga. https://dialnet.unirioja.es/congreso/edicion/10511

Adopting a comprehensive communication approach fosters a closer, more committed relationship between stakeholders and the company within CSR processes and strategies. It prioritizes transparency and moves away from one-sided communication practices, establishing a dialogue-based foundation.[206] Consequently, this enhances one of the most crucial intangible assets in stakeholder-company relations: trust. This strategy deepens engagement and solidifies the mutual understanding and collaboration essential for successful CSR outcomes.

In the marble industry, the dialogue between companies and stakeholders, underpinned by corporate communication, is critical. Through CSR communication, companies offer the public the opportunity to access relevant information if desired, establishing an open line of communication.[207] This accessibility plays a crucial role in maintaining transparency and fostering a relationship of trust and mutual understanding between the marble industry and its varied interest groups.

Long-term planning in CSR communication significantly influences the ability of mining companies to achieve excellence.[208] These companies, along with all other organizations, are realizing that they offer more than just products and services; they also deliver trust and credibility. This effort in communication serves to express the corporate

---

[206] Orozco Toro, J.A., & Ferré Pavia, C. (2013). The strategic communication of corporate social responsibility. *Reason and Word, 83*. Retrieved from http://www.razonypalabra.org.mx/N/N83/V83/20_OrozcoFerre_V83.pdf

[207] Lafuente, A., Viñuales, V., Pueyo, R., & Llaría, J. (2003). *Corporate social responsibility and public policies.* Madrid: Ecology and Development Foundation.

[208] Foote, J., Gaffney, N., & Evans, J.R. (2010). Corporate social responsibility: Implications for performance excellence. *Total Quality Management & Business Excellence, 21*(8), 799-812.

identity (orchestrated through internal communications) that facilitates engagement with external audiences.[209] This is particularly crucial when stakeholders' active engagement online, especially on social media, plays a crucial role in business crises that can damage their reputation and highlight inadequate CSR strategies among some companies. Consequently, these companies must enhance visibility through communication strategies and an active online presence.[210]

Based on the discussion thus far, it's evident that CSR strategies are beyond mere propaganda tools for companies in the marble sector. They are not simply a set of accolades used instrumentally to gain consumer trust. Instead, CSR embodies the systematization and execution of a genuine ethical business vision.[211] The critical attributes of effective CSR communication, regardless of the channel or target audience, include aligning actions with communications both internally and externally; giving priority, where possible, to tangible achievements; highlighting measurable outcomes and concrete results from recent initiatives; and engaging opinion leaders in the development of business strategies. These well-communicated CSR policies balance employees' perceptions of their compensation concerning the social contributions made by the company. Thus, these efforts yield a dual advantage. Firstly, messages about external initiatives from internal sources, such as employees, are perceived

[209] Enrique Jiménez, A.M., & Morales Serrano, F. (2010). Communication and development in the digital age. Paper presented at the AE-IC Congress, University of Malaga. Retrieved from https://dialnet.unirioja.es/congreso/edicion/10511

[210] Orozco Toro, J.A., & Ferré Pavia, C. (2013). The strategic communication of corporate social responsibility. *Reason and Word*, 83. Retrieved from http://www.razonypalabra.org.mx/N/N83/V83/20_OrozcoFerre_V83.pdf

[211] Buyolo García, F. (2015). *Humanizing the company. Towards a new ethical training.* Elche, Spain: Bubok Publishing.

as more credible than broader corporate communications. Secondly, they assist employees in recognizing the importance of supporting sustainable practices to enhance the organization's reputation.[212]

Information about CSR encompasses a wide range of aspects and should be comprehensive, covering all activities along with their significant and easily comprehensible impacts. It should be responsive, communicating in a manner that aligns with the interests of stakeholders and those affected. Additionally, it must be fair and balanced, not disputing the veracity of the data but rather elaborating on it to ensure it is both valuable and relevant. Information should be up-to-date, detailing activities and their timing to facilitate comparisons of current and past actions both within the company and against other organizations. Finally, it should be accessible, ensuring that information on specific areas of interest is readily available to those concerned.[213] Communication is a foundational pillar, enhancing each marble enterprise's strategic framework and corporate ethos by fueling motivation, disseminating information, and fostering community. It enables the transformation of corporate culture via CSR by advocating for ethical integration, spreading exemplary models, and encouraging the adoption of socially responsible practices. This foundation paves the way for the ongoing development of ethical, empathetic, and accountable employees, empowering them to engage with societal issues and the surrounding environment beyond their routine professional duties.[214]

---

[212] Bucur, M., Moica, S., & Fărcaş, R. (2011). The communications of corporate social responsibility-study for ISO 26000. *Scientific Bulletin of the Petru Maior University of Târgu Mureş, 8*(25), 56-59.

[213] Bucur, M., Moica, S., & Fărcaş, R. (2011). The communications of corporate social responsibility-study for ISO 26000. *Scientific Bulletin of the Petru Maior University of Târgu Mureş, 8*(25), 56-59.

[214] Orjuela Córdoba, S. (2011). Communication in the management of corporate social responsibility. *Correspondences & Analysis, 1*, 138-156.

Considering the interplay between communication and strategy means transcending the mere utilitarian actions rooted in pragmatism, situating it within the market's temporal and spatial dimensions and amidst global technological landscapes. This shift brings new settings, stakeholders, and novel forms of interaction at the local and regional levels, which possess significant global impact and challenge worldwide power structures. This evolution in understanding the concept of "communication" moves it beyond a mere operational and tool-based perspective, positioning it as fundamental to an organization's structure and a catalyst for mobilizing its intangible resources. Thus, its role extends far beyond the simplistic view of merely serving as a strategic instrument for sales.[215]

In the context of a marble company, CSR is integral to its communication strategy, guiding its actions, initiatives, and decisions. It fosters strategies designed to establish the company as a trustworthy entity, attractive to investors, and conducive to enhancing the well-being and quality of life for those in its vicinity. Consequently, marble companies that engage in socially responsible practices—as do organizations broadly—garner a more positive reputation, encouraging customer loyalty, instilling pride and a sense of belonging among employees, and earning the confidence of financial markets and governmental bodies.[216] The social and environmental benefits of deploying CSR strategies contribute to a company's responsible and dedicated brand image, amplifying the impact of its communication,

[215] Niño Benavides, T. D. P., & Cortés Cortés, M. I. (2018). Strategic communication and corporate social responsibility, scenarios and potentialities in social capital creation: A literature review. *Prisma Social*, (22), 127–158. https://revistaprismasocial.es/article/view/2570
[216] Briceño, S., Mejías, I., & Moreno, F. (2010). Corporate communication and corporate social responsibility (CSR). *Daena: International Journal of Good Conscience*, 5(1), 37-46.

advertising, and marketing efforts[217] with consumers and stakeholders alike. This is particularly pertinent in times of crisis, such as 2020 to 2022, when consumers demand values and commitment from businesses. Through creative execution, a brand connects to this mission, conveying and sharing its corporate values with the public via innovative concepts and positive imagery.[218]

The report "The Communication of CSR in Spain: Radiography and Diagnosis"[219] underscores that effectively communicating CSR efforts facilitates their solidification and growth, moving beyond skepticism and justification to highlight its core purpose: fostering sustainability and a commitment to the environment and society. A company showcases its expertise and competence by showcasing undertaken initiatives, thereby building credibility in its CSR endeavors and among those who implement them. Communication of CSR is not just an obligation but an essential component of CSR itself and a fundamental aspect of a company's identity. It is deemed vital to cultivate a genuine strategy of relationship-building. Engaging with our stakeholders by sharing values and beliefs fosters connections that strengthen our bond with them. CSR transcends intangible benefits, embodying a company philosophy communicated to and shared with our dialogue partners.

Beyond the intricacies of communicating CSR efforts, a significant challenge for communication strategy leaders

---

[217] Buyolo García, F. (2015). *Humanizing the company. Towards a new ethical training*. Elche, Spain: Bubok Publishing.

[218] Mut Camacho, M., & Breva Franch, E. (2014). CSR communication: Campofrío's strategy. The importance of communication and its interfaces with environmental challenges. *Reason and Word, 79.* https://www.redalyc.org/pdf/1995/199524411041.pdf

[219] Observatory of Communication and Action of Corporate Responsibility. (OCARE, 2015).

is determining the appropriateness of publicizing CSR activities and then deciding on the extent of engagement with stakeholders. The challenge resides in calibrating the degree of this engagement, as overly aggressive promotion of CSR initiatives may be perceived by specific audiences as merely superficial or token gestures.[220]

While the principles discussed here are broadly applicable across industries, the marble sector specifically still grapples with the challenge of CSR communication, debating its appropriateness irrespective of an actual implementation. It's a curious situation where marble companies acknowledge the importance and necessity of adopting proper and suitable CSR practices yet often show reluctance or no intention to communicate these efforts, sometimes even to their stakeholders.[221] In recent years, initiatives like awards and recognitions have been introduced to highlight the efforts of the most dedicated companies in the mining and marble industry, thereby advocating for the role of CSR communication as a valuable tool. The effectiveness of such initiatives in genuinely enhancing the marble sector's dedication to sustainable practices in its economic activities, societal contributions, and environmental protection remains to be seen over time.

---

[220] Orozco Toro, J.A. (2014). Communicate CSR and the impact on the reputation of communication companies: The case of La Marató de TV3 [Doctoral thesis, Autonomous University of Barcelona]. UAB Institutional Repository. https://ddd.uab.cat/record/127044

[221] Viñarás Abad, M., & Niño, J.I. (2019). Public recognition of the communication of corporate social responsibility. In M. González Peláez, M. Valderrama, & A. Various (Eds.), Communicative and persuasive speeches today. Madrid: Tecnos Editorial.

CORPORATE SOCIAL RESPONSIBILITY AS AN INTEGRAL COMMUNICATION STRATEGY FOR MARBLE COMPANIES DURING CRISIS PERIODS

Crisis communication anticipates potential damages to marble companies in extraordinary circumstances that adversely impact their operations, preemptively identifying remedies for the harm incurred. Following the onset of a crisis, it is the responsibility of communication processes and their overseers to navigate and manage the situation.

Mastering communication and maintaining control during any crisis, as well as adeptly managing it, is crucial. Therefore, the communication director (DirCom) needs ample autonomy in decision-making concerning communication strategies to address and mitigate the situation effectively. This role involves crafting communication policies and strategies that align with the organization's objectives and goals, displaying and exercising leadership without manipulation, acting as a spokesperson who effectively conveys and upholds the desired corporate image, and serving as an internal consultant.[222]

The primary aim of crisis communication is to protect and maintain the organization's reputation among its target audiences and within public discourse.[223] This role gained

---

[222] Barbosa Cattani, M. (2014). *Startup comprehensive communication: Communication audit, external and global campaign for the company V y T Indumentaria Médica* [Degree thesis, University of San Francisco de Quito]. USFQ Institutional Repository. https://usfq.edu.ec/handle/23000/3846

[223] European Business and Innovation Center of Galicia. (2009). *Practical manuals for SMEs: How to prepare the communication plan.* Galicia:

immediate significance when the Spanish Government declared a state of alarm on March 14, 2020, marking only the second such occasion in its democratic history—a testament to the gravity of the situation. The COVID-19 pandemic has spotlighted businesses and their obligations to their communities, highlighting their social responsibilities and ability to innovate and adapt during crises. Companies demonstrate their commitment by initiating efforts to mitigate the pandemic's health and social impacts. For these efforts to truly resonate, they must address genuine community needs and be consistent with the company's core mission.

Patricia Meso (2020), who leads the Corporate Communication and Reputation Department at *Hotwire*, *a global communications agency* based in Spain, emphasizes that during alarm and crises—whether health, social, or economic—consumers have heightened expectations for companies and organizations to behave responsibly. Nonetheless, if these responsive actions are not deeply ingrained in a company's core values and ethical guidelines, they risk backfiring. Attempting to gain an advertising edge through such means can prove costly, necessitating extreme care in determining the content and manner of communication. Missteps, especially those perceived as greenwashing,[224] can lead to losing customers.

In 2022, marking the official conclusion of the COVID-19 pandemic, the economic operations of marble companies

---

Business Innovation Center Galicia (BIC). http://cristinaaced.com/pdf/planComunicacion_BIC%20Galicia.pdf

[224] Greenwashing is the term used for practices by companies aimed solely at increasing their profits or sales through green marketing strategies without implementing genuine sustainable management practices. More information can be found at https://www.eco-huella.com/2015/07/greenwashing.html

were significantly disrupted by the crisis, leading to numerous temporary shutdowns and the implementation of temporary employment regulation files (ERTEs).[225] Therefore, as part of their crisis management and/or mitigation plans, these companies must prioritize establishing direct and transparent communication channels with their employees, unions, the media, and public authorities. Until today, marble companies must prioritize human-centric communication strategies in a critical context. The focus should be on protecting jobs and the well-being of employees. While social impact initiatives have traditionally been outward-facing, it's time to look inward, extending beyond corporate volunteerism. The rise in employee layoffs and the broad adoption of ERTEs during Spain's state of alarm highlight the severe challenges facing the Spanish business landscape.[226]

In these challenging times, the most commendable marble companies are those committed to preserving jobs, supplying their workforce with personal protective equipment, enhancing health protocols, and adapting work routines with the help of technology. By establishing guidelines that facilitate remote working, these companies demonstrate a responsible approach to navigating the crisis.

Helena Ancos,[227] the founder of *Ágora*—collective intelligence for sustainability, observes that the COVID-19 pandemic underscores the inseparability of a sustainable economy

---

[225] Royal Decree-Law 8/2020, dated March 17, outlines extraordinary urgent measures to mitigate the economic and social impact of COVID-19.

[226] Andreu Pinillos, A. (2020, April 5). The CSR that will come after COVID-19. *Diario Responsable.* https://diarioresponsable.com/opinion/29103-la-rsc-que-vendra-despues-del-covid-19

[227] Ágora. (n.d.). The effects of COVID-19 on the Sustainable Development Goals. Retrieved from https://www.agorarsc.org/los-efectos-del-covid-19-en-los-objetivos-de-desarrollo-sostenible/

from comprehensive social and health protections. She highlights how environmental and biodiversity crises directly impact sustainable development and the global economy. Ancos sees the crisis as a pivotal opportunity to overhaul the existing economic and social frameworks and advance towards the Sustainable Development Goals set for 2030. To leverage this opportunity effectively, it's crucial to have a thorough understanding of all the communication tools necessary for managing any sensitive situation that could threaten an organization's image and/or reputation.

In crisis management, the necessity for a proficient communication system that operates both internally and externally, including on digital platforms and social media, cannot be overstated. For companies within the marble sector, it's critical to actively monitor and engage with their audience's discourse, develop a response protocol known for its swift and effective reaction to online dynamics, and pursue a communication strategy rooted in transparency, consistency, and accountability towards their stakeholders. Furthermore, assessing and learning from successes and failures is vital for navigating future crises. Continuous monitoring of implemented actions and keeping the audience informed about the company's ongoing concern for the issue are imperative. Additionally, a thorough review of the company's crisis management plan to evaluate the handling of the crisis and the performance of all involved parties is essential for improvement and preparedness for future challenges.[228]

[228] Enrique Jiménez, A.M. (2013). Crisis communication management on social networks. *Orbis. Scientific Journal of Human Sciences, 8*(24), 116-131.

Alicia Cantero (2020),[229] leader of the Political Advocacy Department at *Greenpeace* Spain, emphasizes the significant challenge businesses face in the aftermath of the COVID-19 pandemic, highlighting the imperative need to foster an ecological transition towards a zero-emission society that is resilient and dedicated to conserving and restoring our natural heritage for future generations. This shift will serve as the cornerstone of economic recovery. Investing in and promoting sectors such as renewable energy, the refurbishment of buildings for energy efficiency, demand management, sustainable transport, organic farming, and ecosystem valuation will act as catalysts for job creation. Consequently, it is undeniable that the marble industry must extend its focus beyond merely addressing the immediate issues triggered by the pandemic to developing a post-pandemic action plan that aligns with these broader environmental and societal goals.

[229] Cantero, A. (2020, April 2). COVID-19: A just recovery for people and the environment. Greenpeace España.https://es.greenpeace.org/es/noticias/covid-19-una-recuperacion-justa-para-las-personas-y-el-medioambiente

CONCLUSIONS

This book's investigation into CSR and the communication strategies employed by Spain's mining and marble companies reveals a significant gap in the industry's understanding of its planning and execution. This issue, compounded by the low level of professionalization and the slow adoption of digitalization and technological advancements in the stone market, creates a discouraging scenario. Particularly now, as the industry seeks to recover from the COVID-19 pandemic, the absence of a robust CSR and communication strategy poses a considerable barrier to the marble sector's ability to reach its full potential. The pandemic has catalyzed structural shifts and introduced unforeseen challenges, highlighting companies' need to adapt swiftly and effectively. In the current post-pandemic recovery and adjustment phase, marble businesses in Spain must take immediate and decisive action. Failure to do so will result in increased difficulties in maintaining competitiveness and relevance in a market profoundly altered by the pandemic's economic and social impacts.

While acknowledging the adoption of CSR-related strategies across various facets of marble business management, it's critical to address that these strategies often bear a superficial character, aiming to merely "beautify" advertising efforts with the guise of CSR engagement. Such insincere approaches are fundamentally flawed and can prove to be detrimental. As underscored by the 2009 report on Responsible Communication Strategy and Tools, the exposure of such deceit inflicts considerable harm on the reputation of the implicated business. It's vital to understand that the foundation of a genuinely effective CSR strategy lies in genuine authenticity, transparency, and a sincere dedication to sustainability and social welfare.

The insufficient adoption of CSR and communication strategies over the medium to long term hinders Spanish marble companies from achieving a dual objective: firstly, balancing economic profitability with environmental and social sustainability, and secondly, fortifying their connections with clients, stakeholders, media, industry and environmental entities, academic institutions, specialized centers, public agencies, and society at large. This situation underscores the imperative to acknowledge and integrate all relevant interest groups in formulating and implementing CSR initiatives.

The prevailing job insecurity and ongoing uncertainty, fueled by the COVID-19 pandemic over the past four years, have positioned CSR as an underexplored facet within the business models of marble companies, often perceived more as a financial burden than an opportunity for growth. Despite this, industry leaders cannot overlook the growing influence of consumers on the production and marketing dynamics within the marble sector. Today's consumers demand a business eco-system that champions responsible and sustainable practices that embody CSR's core principles and values. Therefore, it's insufficient for marble companies to focus solely on internal organizational health; they must also contribute to the well-being of the broader social community.[230] The crisis has highlighted the critical need for a comprehensive strategy harmonizing economic, environmental, and social factors to foster a sustainable and robust recovery.

Adopting a CSR framework for marble companies signifies a departure from the traditional business model that has long defined the sector's economic activities. This shift requires harmonizing analog and digital business practices to foster an innovative mindset and embrace a vision of a sustainable, "green future." The persistent inertia found within many marble companies impedes the development and execution of effective CSR and integrated communication strategies, thereby limiting the full utilization of emerging technological advancements.

TECHNOLOGY

The rapid pace of technological advancement is reshaping all aspects of business infrastructure, processes, and market dynamics, significantly impacting CSR and necessitating professionals to consider factors previously overlooked. This includes the technologization of industries, digital market transformation, the need for specialized professional roles, client diversification, intensifying competition, and stricter environmental regulations by governments. Manual or mechanical processes are on the brink of transitioning to digitization and automation. This shift represents a natural progression aligned with structural changes and the

---

[230] Adkins, S. (2004). *Cause Related Marketing: Who Cares Wins*. Oxford: Elsevier Butterworth-Heinemann.

capabilities provided by modern technologies. Such tools not only facilitate the execution of CSR strategies in a more efficient and standardized manner but also become a critical necessity for marble companies aiming to thrive[231] during and after the COVID-19 pandemic crisis.

Technological advancements enable marble companies to optimize human capabilities and natural resources in an efficient and environmentally friendly manner. This is evidenced by the emergence of specialized professional roles and the development of products utilizing recycled materials and industrial waste. Consequently, the frequently cited "resource scarcity" by SME leaders in the marble sector is no longer a viable justification for inactivity and complacency. Large corporations and SMEs must embrace the adoption and strategic execution of CSR initiatives.[232] These smaller entities must recognize that leveraging technological advancements, deploying effective communication strategies, and enacting CSR plans with the help of specialists are crucial factors for the sustainability of their businesses. These actions ensure economic viability and contribute to environmental preservation and societal welfare.

SMALL AND MEDIUM ENTERPRISES (SMES)

The revelation that 99.81% of businesses registered with Social Security in Spain as of August 2023 are SMEs (Strategic Framework in SME Policy 2030, 2023) underscores the pivotal role of small and medium-sized enterprises within the Spanish

---

[231] Carroll, A.B. (2021). Corporate Social Responsibility: Perspectives on the CSR Construct's Development and Future. *Business & Society*, 60(6), 1258-1278.

[232] Jha and Moon (2015) affirm that implementing CSR strategies is more prevalent in large companies.

marble sector. The unique challenges and vulnerabilities SMEs face, stemming from their restricted scale of operations, often result in suboptimal CSR and communication strategies. The tendency among marble companies to view such initiatives as costs rather than investments highlights a significant gap: CSR has yet to become a foundational element of their overall commercial and strategic planning.

Entrepreneurs who adopt a short-sighted and complacent approach are making a critical error. The adoption of a CSR strategy not only catalyzes strategic shifts in SME management within the marble sector—and indeed in larger enterprises—but it also paves the way for novel communication strategies, enhances relationships both internally (between management and employees) and externally (with stakeholders, clients, and institutions), and fosters professional development, specialization, and training within the industry. Such transformations enable marble companies to seamlessly align with societal and environmental demands while achieving economic success. Despite the myriad benefits associated with CSR, a segment of the marble industry persists in clinging to outdated operational methods, resisting the shift towards sustainable development. This reluctance is often linked to a failure to adapt to the digital landscape among CSR and communication leaders within SMEs. Many professionals, who might be generalists or misplaced, utilize digital tools—such as websites and social media—at a level more akin to lay users than that of experts. This scenario results in SMEs within the marble industry transitioning towards sustainable and digital business models in a haphazard, reluctant, and belated manner.

Adopting a strategic and organized approach to CSR eliminates the reliance on short-term planning, imbalances, and disarray.

The commitments made by all marble companies, particularly SMEs, towards the sustainable development of their business models, are intrinsically connected to the local environments and ecosystems they inhabit. Consequently, their products' quality and potential for expansion are intimately tied to the CSR initiatives that, in various ways, impact the communities they serve.

Compared to their larger counterparts, one significant challenge for SMEs in the marble sector is their limited access to human, technological, and financial resources needed to adapt to CSR changes effectively. However, the core issue plaguing the marble industry is the fragmentation of businesses and a lack of unified effort. Dominated by SMEs, the industry's failure to foster commercial and social cooperation and forge internal consensus renders it vulnerable to external pressures and ill-equipped to navigate crises such as COVID-19. Presenting an illusion of normalcy and unity amidst such high-risk and precarious circumstances could be detrimental. The sector's strategy should focus on adopting sustainability initiatives capable of weathering the storm and emerging stronger post-COVID-19. This necessitates a well-crafted contingency or crisis management plan. The coming months will serve as a critical juncture to observe whether marble companies truly embrace their CSR commitments, demon-strating the ability to collaborate and support one another as a cohesive industry.

The ongoing health, social, and economic upheavals instigated by COVID-19 precipitate significant, lasting changes within the marble industry. This "new reality," compounded by rapid technological evolution and the pressure of mandatory legislative and regulatory adjustments, presents Spanish marble business leaders with formidable challenges, placing many at a crossroads. The time has come to move beyond merely applying stopgap solutions to the increasingly outdated marble business model and to begin crafting an industry that aligns with the current landscape. Thus, Spanish marble companies' critical tasks include addressing urgent economic concerns, restructuring, modernizing, aligning their operations with CSR legislative requirements, and pursuing consolidation and exploration of new markets.

The COVID-19 pandemic has catalyzed widespread, enduring, and permanent[233] transformations within the marble industry, merging with technological advancements and a complex array of obligatory legislative and regulatory mandates. This confluence of factors significantly strains Spanish marble entrepreneurs, threatening to expose numerous businesses and their leaders to scrutiny. It has become imperative to move beyond makeshift solutions to the deep-seated issues within the traditional marble business model and initiate the development of an industry that resonates with the current reality. Consequently, the principal obligations of Spanish marble firms encompass tackling urgent economic challenges, undergoing comprehensive restructuring, modernizing and aligning operations with CSR legislative requirements, and striving to stabilize and penetrate new markets.

Investing in CSR involves not just financial but also human resources. Consequently, such investments should extend beyond tangible assets to increasingly address intangible factors. Legislatively, the Spanish marble sector is confronted with a Global Restoration Plan and a Waste Management

[233] Carroll, A.B. (2021). Corporate Social Responsibility: Perspectives on the CSR Construct's Development and Future. *Business & Society*, 60(6), 1258-1278.

Plan, mandating businesses to align their operations with the guidelines established in Royal Decree 975/2009 concerning CSR.

In the marble industry, companies prioritize developing and reinforcing their economic and financial plans, often relegating CSR and communication strategies to a secondary status. This approach is fundamentally flawed because CSR initiatives are far from being merely altruistic gestures. Instead, they are integral to bolstering communication and marketing strategies, serving as a stabilizing force amidst the erosion of traditional markets, whether from natural market cycles or periods of crisis, and crucial for carving out new market opportunities.

CSR communication within marble companies advocates for more transparent business operations, a crucial factor in enhancing trust and assurance among clients, internal and external stakeholders, and various institutions, especially during times of uncertainty and crisis. Thus, providing easy access to legal and regulatory information for all interested parties, delivering clear and precise information about the company's internal operations, and showcasing its CSR initiatives are vital steps toward establishing a brand identity founded on ethical and responsible values toward the eco-system and community where it operates.

While marble business owners are beginning to recognize the growing importance of communication, embracing the notion that "if it's not communicated, it doesn't exist," the reality remains that, apart from a few notable exceptions among the largest firms, SMEs typically lack a structured communication strategy, let alone a CSR initiative. New business and consumption practices emerge in a continuously changing marketplace marked by escalating competition and profound health, social, and economic challenges. These practices adhere to standards promoting the sustainability of the environment and the community.

PROFESSIONALIZATION

The marble sector recognizes the necessity for enhanced professionalization, a sentiment its workforce echoes. Corporate Social Responsibility (CSR) may be emerging within the Spanish market, but it boasts a substantial legacy in markets with higher levels of professional maturity.[234] Spain's marble industry suffers from a deficiency in professionalization. This factor hampers the development of union consciousness and collaborative efforts to achieve collective benefits that span economic, social, and environmental realms.

In the aftermath of COVID-19, it has become crucial for the industry to embrace sustainable practices and incorporate cutting-edge technologies. Shifting towards a circular economy and adopting sustainable manufacturing methods are imperative to reduce environmental impact and cater to the increasing consumer appetite for eco-friendly products. Digital transformation should target not just

---

[234] Hewlett-Packard (HP), founded by William "Bill" Redington Hewlett and David "Dave" Packard in 1939 in Palo Alto, California, is a prominent business example of innovation, adaptability, and corporate social responsibility (CSR). Focused initially on electronic instrumentation, HP expanded to become a global leader in information technology. In 2015, the company strategically split into Hewlett Packard Enterprise (HPE), specializing in business solutions, and HP Inc., focused on printers and PCs, demonstrating its adaptability. HP has pioneered sustainability initiatives, education, and community well-being, working on reducing its carbon footprint and promoting diversity and inclusion. These efforts have strengthened its corporate image and significantly contributed to its long-term success.

the enhancement of operational efficiency but also the bolstering of supply chain traceability and transparency. Blockchain and artificial intelligence can enhance customer and stakeholder trust by adding value. Moreover, ongoing education and professional growth within the industry should expand beyond technical competencies to include insights on sustainability, business ethics, and innovation. This approach will boost the industry's competitiveness and fortify its corporate reputation.

For the successful execution of CSR initiatives and holistic communication strategies over the medium to long term, it's essential to establish tangible and virtual infrastructures—ranging from manufacturing sites and extraction locations to websites and digital platforms. Moreover, the processes governing these structures should be managed by professionals with the necessary expertise and training, including Directors of Communication, CSR experts, IT and robotics specialists, and marketing leaders. This approach enables industries to effectively leverage digitalization, data integration, and robotics technologies, which are crucial in the contemporary market landscape.

BREAKPOINTS

It's important to underscore the growing divide between the private marble industry and public entities. This widening rift has exacerbated the negative impacts of market downturns and recurrent economic challenges. Although governmental efforts may seem inadequate, marble enterprises must be well-informed about CSR-related regulations and the public sector's initiatives. This includes understanding and accessing available support, such as the Ministry for the

Ecological Transition grants to enhance safety, environmental standards, and sustainability, especially targeting SMEs. Additionally, firms should be aware of funding opportunities from the European *Next Generation EU* Recovery Funds, overseen by the Ministries of Ecological Transition and the Demographic Challenge, as well as initiatives designed to mitigate the effects of COVID-19 initiated in May 2021.

This perspective does not aim to cast the relationship between marble industry leaders and public administrators in terms of right or wrong. Instead, it emphasizes that the discord between the two does not serve either party's interests. Both sides must work towards an agreement or, at the very least, a consensus. Such collaboration would ensure the marble sector's economic prosperity and uphold environmental conservation and community engagement commitments.

The examination proposed in this book sheds light on the intricate landscape Spanish marble enterprises navigate concerning CSR and communication efforts. The journey towards genuine and impactful CSR is fraught with challenges, yet it remains a pivotal endeavor for the sector's sustainable evolution. Echoing the sentiments of António Guterres, UN Secretary-General, during World Population Day, we are reminded to appreciate our diversity, acknowledge our shared humanity, and reflect on the health advancements that have significantly improved life expectancy and decreased maternal and child mortality. His words also prompt a collective obligation to protect our planet and intro-spect on our unmet pledges to one another. This message is profoundly aligned with the essence of this book, advocating for the marble industry's crucial role in fostering a future that is both sustainable and ethically responsible.

The discussions and analysis within these pages, particularly against the backdrop of the rapidly shifting global scenario as evidenced by deliberations at the 54th World Economic Forum in Davos (Switzerland), resonate with the themes of this study. The focus on artificial intelligence management and the call for governance that champions transparency and inclusivity underscore the technological advancements impacting the marble industry. Such evolution is vital for enhancing operational efficiency and bolstering sustainability efforts, further emphasizing the sector's responsibility towards adopting more responsible business practices and communication strategies.

In June 2024, the United Nations released a report[235] highlighting the severity of the ongoing climate crisis. The report emphasized that 2023 was the hottest year, with global temperatures increasing alarmingly. This trend is primarily attributed to human activities, including burning fossil fuels, deforestation, and unsustainable agricultural practices. The UN called on all countries to intensify their efforts to reduce emissions and adopt more drastic measures to mitigate climate change.

For the marble industry in Spain, embracing eco-friendly and "green" practices and contributing to the circular and *spiral economies*[236] are pivotal elements of Corporate Social Responsibility. The sector must synchronize with these worldwide challenges to guarantee long-term sustainability and commitment to environmental stewardship.

---

[235] United Nations. (2024, June 29). The UN raises an alarm about the global climate crisis. UN News. https://news.un.org/es/story/2024/06/1530871

[236] Oller Alonso, M., & Oller Alonso, M. (forthcoming). From the "circular fallacy" to the (r)evolution of the spiral economy.

WEB PAGES RELATED TO CSR EXAMINED FOR THIS BOOK

- AENOR: https://www.aenor.com/
- Agora: Collective Intelligence for Sustainability: https://www.agorarsc.org/
- Almanzora.Ideal.es: https://almanzora.ideal.es/
- National Association of Aggregate Manufacturers (ANEFA): https://www.aridos.org/
- BBVA: https://www.bbva.com/
- Virtual Library on Social Responsibility and related topics: http://www.bibliotecavirtualrs.com/
- Official Bulletin of the Junta de Andalucía: https://www.juntadeandalucia.es/boja/
- State Official Bulletin: https://www.boe.es/
- Canvas, strategic consulting specialized in corporate social responsibility: https://www.canvasconsultores.com/coronavirus-empresas/
- Marble Stone and Materials Technology Center: https://ctmarmol.es/
- World Business Council for Sustainable Development: https://www.wbcsd.org/
- Cosentino S.A.: https://www.cosentino.com
- Cuellar Stone: http://www.cuellarstone.com/
- Human Rights: https://www.humanrights.ch/de/
- Economista.es: https://www.eleconomista.es/
- Access to European Union Law: https://eur-lex.europa.eu/
- El Español.com: https://www.elespanol.com/
- El País: https://elpais.com
- The Natural Step: https://thenaturalstep.org/
- Cosentino Corporate School: https://www.elearningcosentino.com/
- GRI Standards: https://www.globalreporting.org/

- Europapress.es: https://www.europapress.es/andalucia/
- Finanzas.com: http://www.finanzas.com/
- Forética: http://foretica.org/
- Spanish Forum for Socially Responsible Investment (SPAINSIF): http://www.mitramiss.gob.es/es/rse/inversion/index.htm
- Foundation for Value Reports, Integrated Reports: https://integratedreporting.org/
- Infoayudas. Subsidies within your reach: https://www.infoayudas.com/
- Institute of Hydrology, Meteorology and Environmental Studies: http://www.ideam.gov.co/web/atencion-y-participacion-ciudadana/cambio-climatico
- Junta de Andalucía: https://www.juntadeandalucia.es
- La Vanguardia: https://www.lavanguardia.com
- Macael Tourism: https://macaelturismo.com/
- Ministry of Foreign Affairs, European Union and Cooperation: http://www.exteriores.gob.es/
- Ministry of Social Rights and 2030 Agenda: https://www.agenda2030.gob.es/
- Ministry of Labour, Migrations and Social Security of Spain: http://www.mitramiss.gob.es
- Spanish Ministry of Employment and Social Security: http://www.mitramiss.gob.es/
- Ministry for the Ecological Transition and the Demographic Challenge: https://www.miteco.gob.es/
- Monografías.com: https://www.monografias.com/
- United Nations: https://www.un.org/
- United Nations Human Rights Office of the High Commissioner: https://www.ohchr.org/
- ISO 14001:2015 Standard: https://www.nueva-iso-14001.com/
- OMYA: https://www.omya.com/

- International Organization for Standardization: https://www.iso.org/
- International Labour Organization: https://www.ilo.org/global/lang—es/index.htm
- Organization for Economic Co-operation and Development: http://mneguidelines.oecd.org/
- Global Compact. Spanish Network: https://www.pactomundial.org/
- Digital newspaper Focus Piedra: https://www.focuspiedra.com/
- Incorpora Program: https://www.incorpora.org/
- Provencale: https://www.provencale.com/
- Waste Professional: https://www.residuos-profesional.com/
- Accountability: https://www.accountability.org/
- RSC Cosentino: https://rsc.cosentino.com/
- RSC Cosentino 2018: https://assetstools.cosentino.com/api/v1/bynder/doc/E918B386-8332-4C03-A59DF-CB818084A07/Cosentino-RSC18-ES
- RSC Cosentino 2019: https://www.cosentino.com/es/wp-content/uploads/2020/07/RSC-2019-ESP-VDIGITAL-v3-E.pdf
- RSC Cosentino 2020: https://rsc.cosentino.com/wp-content/uploads/2021/06/Cosentino-RSC-2020-ES_-Digital.pdf
- SlideShare from Scribd: https://es.slideshare.net/
- Social Accountability International: https://sa-intl.org/
- Foreign Trade Society of Peru: https://www.comexperu.org.pe/
- AntConc Software: http://www.laurenceanthony.net/software/antconc/
- Technological Solution for Governance, Risk, and Compliance Management: https://www.isotools.org/